FORBIDDEN CITY

FORBIDDEN CITY

THE GREAT WITHIN

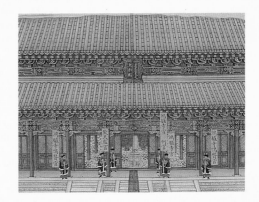

MAY HOLDSWORTH

AND

CAROLINE COURTAULD

PHOTOGRAPHY BY HU CHUI

Text © 2008, 1998, 1995 May Holdsworth
and Caroline Courtauld
Photographs © Hu Chui
and the Palace Museum, Beijing

First published in 1995
in Hong Kong by Odyssey Publications Ltd.

This paperback edition published in 2008 by
Odyssey Books & Guides
903 Seaview Commercial Building
21–24 Connaught Road West
Hong Kong
www.odysseypublications.com

ISBN 978-962-217-792-5
Library of Congress Catalog Card Number
has been requested.

Distributed in the USA by
W.W. Norton & Company, Inc.
500 Fifth Avenue
New York, NY 10110
USA
www.wwnorton.com

5 7 9 10 8 6 4

Designed by New Strategy Limited

Printed in China by
1010 Printing International Limited

CONTENTS

ACKNOWLEDGEMENTS

This book was published in tandem with a documentary film of the same title made by Totem Film Productions and produced and directed by Francis Gerard.

Illustration Credits

(Page 33) Copyright British Museum. (Pages 36, 44-45, 49, 140) Courtesy of the Palace Museum, Taipei. (Pages 47, 126) Courtesy of Mary Evans Picture Library. (Page 51) Courtesy of the Royal Geographical Society. (Page 63, bottom) Courtesy of the First Historical Archives of China, Beijing. (Page 102) © Photo Réunion des Musées Nationaux. (Pages 111, 112-13, 116-17) Courtesy of Martyn Gregory Gallery. (Page 115) The Royal Archives © Her Majesty Queen Elizabeth II. (Page 118) Courtesy of the British Library. (Pages 122, top and bottom; 123) Courtesy of Hong Kong Museum of Art. (Page 124) Bequest of Grenville L. Winthrop. Courtesy of the Fogg Art Museum, Harvard University. (Pages 127, 142) Courtesy of The Illustrated London News. (Page 132, top and bottom) Courtesy of Totem Film Productions (Hong Kong) Ltd. (Pages 134-35) Courtesy of the Percival David Foundation of Chinese Art. (Page 137) Courtesy of Lay Pheng Teo. (Page 143) Courtesy of Niu Chen.

All other illustrations are reproduced by courtesy of the Palace Museum, Beijing.

Captions to photographs on preceding pages

(Pages 2-3) Courtiers in front of the Hall of Supreme Harmony, from The Grand Imperial Wedding, an album of paintings recording the wedding of emperor Guangxu. (Pages 4-5) The Hall of Central Harmony, on a terrace of white marble. The dragon heads, functioning as water spouts when it rains, are part of the drainage system. (Pages 6-7) Interior walls of the Forbidden City. (Pages 8-9) Demonstration of equestrian skills by the soldiers of the Eight Banners, painted by Giuseppe Castiglione and others. (This page) Watchtower and moat. (Endpapers) Ice-skating, by Jin Kun.

MAP OF THE FORBIDDEN CITY

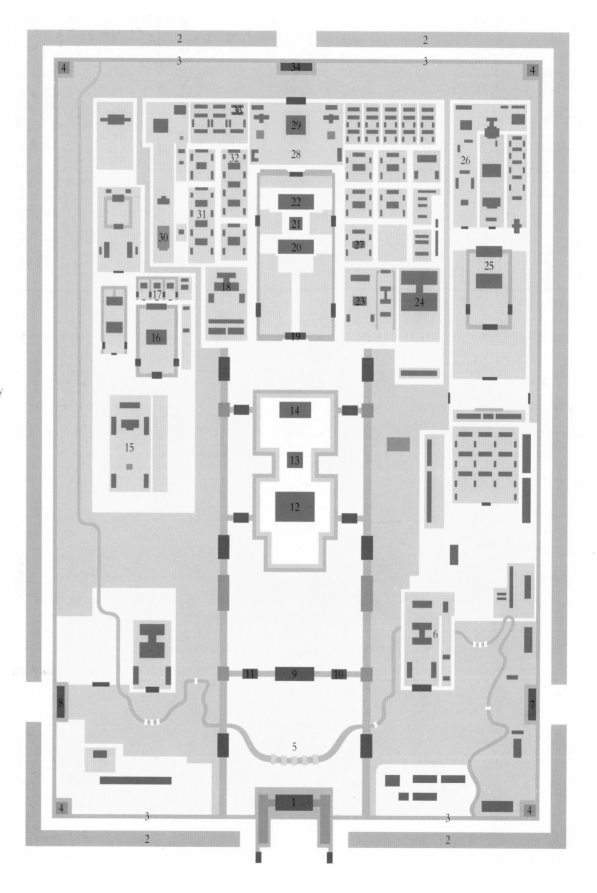

FOREWORD

The Forbidden City at the heart of Beijing is China's largest and most well-preserved palace complex from antiquity, a living monument to China's tradition of imperial architecture. Twenty-four emperors of the Ming and Qing dynasties (1368-1911) lived here. Reflecting principles based on long-held beliefs of the ceremonial and cosmological importance of the imperial role, the architecture of this magnificent palace embodies elements relating to the strict hierarchy prevalent in feudal times as well as assumptions about an emperor's omnipotence. It was built also to provide the sort of extravagant lifestyle demanded by the imperial family.

According to the *Shijing*, China's earliest collection of poetry compiled by Confucius, "there is no land on earth that is not the monarch's, nor are there people within its boundaries who are not his subjects." Since emperors traditionally regarded all territory and indeed all mankind as their personal possessions, it was a matter of course that the Palace drew the best craftsmen and artists, and collected tribute ranging from the most outstanding works of art to the rarest exotica. The connoisseurship of the emperors Kangxi and Qianlong, especially, turned this Palace into a treasure house of the finest creations of Chinese culture.

In 1925, sometime after the fall of the Qing dynasty, the Forbidden City was established as a museum, and the previously hidden treasures were at last shown to the public. Today domestic and international visitors to the Palace Museum number several million every year.

The ancient civilization of China remains a mystery to many, and for Westerners perhaps the most intriguing enigma is still the secluded life of the former emperors in the Forbidden City. The sort of questions most frequently asked are: how did this "Heaven-blest" being, this emperor, rule his vast territory and his countless subjects? what were his everyday concerns? what was done for such events as marriage or death? did he enjoy studying or some other forms of recreation? what was in fact the extent of the rare works and exotica collected under his patronage? Given China's very long history, ancient civilization, and the barriers posed by language, any attempt to unravel the enigma is usually fraught with difficulty. But for those readers interested in making the attempt, I am now pleased to be able to recommend this guide, *Forbidden City: The Great Within*, and also on behalf of my colleagues to salute and thank all those who have brought it into being.

楊 新

YANG XIN
Deputy Director of the Palace Museum

INTRODUCTION

JONATHAN D. SPENCE

For almost exactly five hundred years, from early in the Ming dynasty until the fall of the Qing in 1912, the Forbidden City in Beijing served as the locus and symbol of Chinese imperial power. The initial decision made by the Ming emperor Yongle (reigned 1403-24) in 1403 to relocate his capital there was based partly on strategic considerations, and partly out of sentiment for the days of his youth, when as the Prince of Yan he had lived in the city known at that time as Beiping, or "Northern Peace." Furthermore, as a usurper who had only won the throne after a murderous and protracted civil war, Yongle had little wish to keep his capital in the city of Nanjing, far to the south, where his father had first formed the new dynasty in 1368.

Though the capital and palaces of the former Mongol Yuan dynasty were near the site of the present city, the vast palace complex that we know today, and its spatial location within the town that surrounds it, were very much the fruit of Yongle and his architects. In 1420 Yongle considered the city far enough along to rename it Beijing, or "Northern Capital," and to start holding court ceremonials there. One of the sons of the great central Asian ruler Timur visited the growing city in 1420, and wrote in awe of its colossal size, and the vast courtyard of dressed stone that stretched for "seven hundred paces" in front of the main palace entrance. But he noted that the city was not yet completed, since more than one hundred thousand poles of scaffolding were still in

(Pages 14-15) Imperial Garden. (Opposite) Formal portrait of emperor Kangxi. (Above) Dragon motif on an emperor's court robe.

place at the site, and in order to be received in audience by the Ming emperor he had to pass through an outer gate tower that was still under construction.

Yongle died in 1424, and was buried early the next year in the magnificent mausoleum he had erected on the edge of the mountains twenty-six miles to the north of the imperial city, the first and grandest of that area of Ming tombs that is today one of China's foremost tourist attractions. It was half a millennium later, in 1925, that the Forbidden City itself was opened as the newly named Palace Museum, after the forced eviction of the Manchu Puyi (reigned 1909-12), China's last emperor. Puyi had abdicated the throne in 1912, at the age of six, after another civil war (though one somewhat less bloody than that fought by his eminent predecessor) had ended the Manchu dynasty. During that intervening decade Puyi had been permitted to continue living in the Palace — with a large government stipend to pay the costs of the still enormous imperial household — under an agreement worked out for him by his imperial relatives and the rulers of the newly formed Chinese Republic.

In the long span of time between the early fifteenth century and the early twentieth, the halls and palaces of the Forbidden City had slowly filled with the loot and the tribute gifts from scores of military campaigns and hundreds of foreign embassies, as well as with the "gifts" — enforced or voluntary — from countless ministers, provincial officials, wealthy scholars, and merchants: carvings of jade, ivory and scented wood, vessels of gold and bronze, porcelain receptacles of every conceivable shape and size, embroidered fabrics and silks from the imperial looms, intricate mechanical toys and bejeweled watches from Europe's finest craftsmen, portraits of ancestors and distinguished ministers and generals, painted panoramas of the imperial army's greatest battles or the emperors' grandest tours across their realm, rugs of wool and silk, incense burners, rich wall hangings and gleaming furniture, all mixed in wild profusion in the latticed and colonnaded buildings that stood symmetrically placed inside the wide expanses of the palace grounds. The accumulation went on and on despite the erection of other palaces, as large or larger, in neighboring or distant areas, most spectacularly the sprawling summer palace in the hills and on the waterfront of the scenic lakes to the west of Beijing, or the Manchu emperors' more northerly palaces in Rehe (Jehol), where they could escape the pressures and heat of the city to hunt in the open country, and receive the emissaries from the Mongol tribes and central Asia.

The ever-dreaded threat of fire hung at all times across the Forbidden City, and sometimes took its toll, though fire-

prevention was a constant concern of the emperors, and seems to have been remarkably effective. War, too, intruded on occasion, though surprisingly rarely given the long time-span we are considering. In 1644, when Beijing was seized by the peasant troops of the rebel leader Li Zicheng, and the last Ming emperor hanged himself in the Imperial Garden, there was some looting and destruction, but most of the palaces and their contents survived, to be taken over almost at once, and re-sequestered, by the self-appointed Manchu rulers of the new Qing dynasty. A handful of rebels entered the palace grounds in 1813, but were quickly rounded up by palace guards and killed. The

troops of the French and British expeditionary force, commanded by Lord Elgin, skirted the area in 1860, but contented themselves with burning the summer palace of Yuanmingyuan. In 1900 another, larger, expeditionary force of Western and Japanese troops entered Beijing to raise the Boxer siege of the foreign legations; they quartered themselves and their horses in the edges of the Forbidden City for close to a year, but left most of the palaces intact.

The 1912 revolution saw remarkably little vandalism of the Forbidden City, though in the twilight years of Puyi's abdication many precious objects were spirited out of the Palace by Puyi's eunuch staff, and perhaps by the ex-emperor's own relatives, and were sold on the open market to art dealers who gathered in Beijing from around the world in those years. During a brief imperial restoration attempt by a pro-Manchu warlord general in 1917, the Forbidden City received its first and only aerial bombing, but the damage fortunately was slight. When another warlord forced Puyi out of the Palace in the 1920s, again some of the treasures were lost, but the main destruction then and in the ensuing years was of the vast stores of archival documents of the Ming and Qing dynasties, which moldered in their leaking palace storerooms, or were sold on the streets of Beijing for fuel or wrapping paper. The Japanese, who controlled the city between 1938 and 1945, left the Palace undisturbed. And though in 1948 and 1949 the retreating forces of the Nationalist Guomindang sent many of the palace treasures to Taiwan to boost the prestige of their regime-in-exile, they concentrated mainly on the rarer paintings, and on the surviving archives that would help them to write the history of the fallen Qing. Despite these varying crises, the core of the palace collections remained virtually intact in all their astonishing variety, as this volume so triumphantly demonstrates.

The Forbidden City has been a central focus of the Western fascination with China ever since Matteo Ricci first entered its outer gates in 1601, to pay homage to the invisible emperor's empty throne, and when first-hand knowledge was lacking, imagination and speculation filled the gap. The two most powerful evocations of this sense of awe and mystery were provided by two Western writers just after the

years." For to Kafka this was "the center of the world," yes, but also a place "crammed to bursting with its own sediment."

To Kafka's contemporary, the French poet, novelist, and art historian Victor Segalen, the mystery lay even deeper than this. For beneath the visible city, around which one could ride in the dawn air, and the roofs of which one could see glimmering yellow above the curtaining walls, there lay another city one could only sense, the existence of which was proven by the hollow sound that occasionally reverberated under one's horse's hooves. This other city, this "true"

(Left) Gold Buddha figure, from the relics collection of the Palace Museum. (Above) Triumphal entry into Beijing, part of twelve scrolls on Emperor Kangxi's Tour of the South, painted by Wang Hui and others.

fall of the Qing dynasty, but before the Palace was opened to the world's gaze. In his beautiful and enigmatic parable *The Great Wall of China* Franz Kafka sees the Palace world as one of endlessly receding perimeters, so that even the most determined messenger can never get through all the layers before him to carry the emperors' real message to the outside world. In this bleak and vibrant vision, even if the messenger could get "through the chambers of the innermost palace . . . nothing would be gained; the courts would still have to be crossed; and after the courts the second outer palace; and once more stairs and courts; and once more another palace; and so on for thousands of

Forbidden City, was "not, as one might think, a chessboard whose game, fair or foul, is played on the surface. No — there is an Underground City complete with its redans, its corner forts, its highways and byways, its approaches, its threats, its 'horizontal wells' even more formidable than the wells of drinking and other water that yawn up at the open sky." So it is, for the protagonist in Segalen's story, that this other Forbidden City "has suddenly opened up other Palaces of Dreams whose passages I am far from having trodden!"

Now, some eighty years after those two sets of lines were written, and eighty years after the contents of the Forbidden City were first displayed to the world, this richly layered volume permits us to ruminate at leisure on the mass of objects and their histories, and encourages us to plumb what lies behind the triple mysteries of their creation, their accumulation, and their survival.

OUTER COURT

Heaven, protecting the inferior people, has constituted for them rulers and teachers,

who should be able to be assisting to God, extending favor and producing

tranquility throughout all parts of the kingdom.

Shujing (or *The Book of History*)

Emperor Yongle's Dream of Red Mansions

This is the story of a palace, the Forbidden City, the largest surviving monument to China's imperial past. It is not told in strict chronological sequence, but proceeds along the line of an imaginary Imperial Way, from court to court and hall to hall rather than from one historical period to another. But to start our story from the very beginning, we do have to make one leap back in time, to a moment just over six hundred years ago, when Yongle became the emperor of China.

Yongle was a younger son of Zhu Yuanzhang, conqueror of the Mongols and founder of the Ming dynasty (1368-1644). When Zhu Yuanzhang died, the throne passed to a grandson, but Yongle commanded a powerful regional army; marching at the head of it, he unleashed a civil war to ensure that his nephew's reign was brief. Proclaiming himself emperor, he moved swiftly to consolidate his control and then began planning his new capital. It was to be moved from Nanjing, the dynastic capital on the Yangzi River, to his own power base in the north, a site within riding distance of a sweep of the Great Wall. There he would erect his palace at the spot where Kublai Khan had set his winter capital Khanbalik in 1267.

The Mongols were not the first nomads to invade China, nor would they be the last. The northern border had always been vulnerable. Two centuries before Christ, China had been unified for the first time by a great warrior. He linked up a broken line of

(Pages 20-21) Glazed figures of beasts on a roof ridge. (Opposite) Emperor Yongle. (Above) Watchtower at one of the four corners of the walled Palace.

fortifications across the empire's northern frontier to create a stupendous defensive barrier against the nomadic cattle-raisers of the steppes. The Great Wall separated the agrarian from the pastoral way of life and for centuries provided the most tangible definition of the Chinese cultural world — all those living beyond it were considered barbarians. From today's standpoint, the Great Wall might be seen as both an icon of

China's ancient civilization and a symbol of the inwardness and isolation that has characterized so much of her history.

The new capital Beijing, partially erected on the foundations of Khanbalik, was planned on a scale befitting the confidence and dynamism of the dynasty that had liberated China from the Mongols. Yongle saw in his mind's eye a splendid shining city rising out of the dusty North China Plain, built in a series of concentric rectangles that would be as orderly as he intended his empire to be. The first of the rectangles delineated an Inner City, which was girded by a defensive perimeter wall; within it was the Imperial City, itself moated and walled and entered by the Gate of Heavenly Peace (Tiananmen); then, at the heart of it all, stood the innermost walled rectangle we know as the Forbidden City — a city of walls within walls within walls. It was little wonder that the Palace came to be known as *Da Nei*, the Great Within. Later, during the reign of the emperor Jiajing (1522-66), another city wall was added enclosing the southern suburbs (Outer City). This layout remained basically unchanged until the end of the Qing dynasty in 1911-12.

The principal streets of Ming Beijing formed a grid; straight thoroughfares paralleled and intersected one another, and most of the major buildings were placed on the north-south axis, the meridian line, or on either side of it. Thus the Forbidden City lay directly on the axis, while the Temple of Heaven, also constructed in Yongle's reign, and the Temple of Agriculture, built by Jiajing, were located east and west of the line. Completing the symmetrical layout, Jiajing built the Altars of the Earth, Sun and Moon at the other cardinal points — north, east and west. "The symmetry of the capital city (indeed, of most Chinese cities in varying degrees) reflects the sociopolitical ideal: balanced, stable, hierarchical, harmonious."[1]

Ancient cosmological and geomantic principles were applied to bring the most auspicious influences into play. Since time immemorial, the choice of a new site for a dwelling or a grave had always been dictated by considerations of *fengshui,* a form of divination based on the idea that there were felicitous and baleful influences in the natural environment which could be harnessed or evaded if certain rules were followed. These rules were intricately linked to the cardinal points, of which there were five (the center, south, east, west and north, in order of auspiciousness), and to a set of numbers, of which nine was the most highly regarded. Not surprisingly, therefore, Yongle's palace faced south, with gates positioned in the walls on the four cardinal points. Within it various architectural features were arranged

in sets of nine; the golden bosses on the huge red doors, for instance, total eighty-one or nine times nine.

How perfect *fengshui* was achieved for the Forbidden City is explained by the following story. It seems that Yongle was advised by an astrologer, Liu Bowen, who had drawn a blueprint in which spaces and buildings in the new city were related to parts of the human body. To cite a few examples from this plan, the central south gateway to the Inner City, Qianmen, was the head; the Imperial Way represented the windpipe; the Gate of Heavenly Peace was the pericardium; the Meridian Gate (Wumen) the heart; the Hall of Supreme Harmony (Taihedian) stood for a duct which according to the Chinese connected the heart and the liver; and the Palace of Heavenly Purity (Qianqinggong) symbolized an anatomical point between the kidneys believed to be a fatal spot.[2]

Besides geomantic considerations, the architecture of the Forbidden City was also shaped by a belief in the cosmic significance of the imperial office. From earliest times, the emperor had been regarded as rather more than human; he was the Son of Heaven, and his conduct had a direct bearing on keeping the delicate balance between the earthly and cosmic orders. Even the Chinese name of his palace, Zijincheng (Purple Forbidden City), embodied an allusion to the Pole Star, a celestial metaphor for the emperor's pivotal role in the terrestrial world.

To express the desired balance, the same symmetrical precision evident in the plan of the capital city was adopted, and indeed a particular quality of the Forbidden City is its serenity. A visitor's first impression may be that of solidity — the architecture seems one of mass, right angles and exaggerated proportions. But another impression soon takes over: by marooning the great buildings in immense space, in wide courts of flagstones, the architects somehow endowed the Palace with not just grandeur and majesty, but also a transcendental calm.

A million workmen and one hundred thousand artisans turned Yongle's dream into reality. The empire was scoured for the finest materials. Timber from the southwestern provinces was floated thousands of miles for the richly lacquered columns of the resplendent halls. Kilns were set up in Beijing's surrounding countryside to fire the bricks and yellow tiles laid on the walls and roofs. A single piece of marble, 250 tons in weight, was transported from the suburbs in winter so that it could be hauled over a route frozen by water drawn from wells dug every third mile. Craftsmen from throughout the land came to carve, paint and decorate the beams, ceilings and pillars, setting them ablaze with the gorgeous coloring of gold, red, blue and green. By 1420 Yongle's capital was basically completed, and he formally moved his court there in 1421. Twenty-three emperors spanning nearly five hundred years ruled from this Palace after him.

The centuries have naturally taken their toll; most of the buildings have been rebuilt and repaired many times, and indeed restoration continues today. If anything, the effect of dust and age on the Forbidden City has added to its picturesqueness, and it is especially beautiful under fresh snow, when the blood red of the walls is tempered by drifts of dazzling white. Yet it is on another kind of winter's day, when pale sunshine falls in dusty shafts on the empty squares, that the Palace seems at its most timeless and impersonal, a world away from the knots of vendors, visitors and cars clustered outside. Half-closing your eyes, you might see not just the expanses of white and red but perhaps a stately yellow parasol or the sheen of an embroidered dragon on a blue satin sleeve, as a procession led by the emperor's jade coach sways toward the central tunnel of the Meridian Gate, to disappear behind the studded doors of the Forbidden City.

Imagine also, as you lift your eyes up to the gate-towers, how an earlier visitor might have trembled in the very same spot, and felt the threatening strength and power emanating from those high blank walls. That previous visitor, traveling from the south, would already have passed through four sets of gates to reach the Imperial City, until his way along a wall-enclosed corridor was barred by

A corner of the Palace in winter.

the Upright Gate (Duanmen) and beyond it, at the end of another enclosure, by the massive Meridian Gate.

"One can well imagine the growing bewilderment and disquiet of such a person as he passed through one blank wall and beneath one brooding gate-house after another, to find beyond it only a featureless avenue leading to yet another wall and gate. Reality was softening into a dream. His mind, so long attentive to a distant goal somewhere ahead in this labyrinth of straight lines, so long expecting a climax that never seemed to come, must at last have refused to record and memorise the minor differences in scale, proportion, and decorative detail of the buildings that were the only landmarks of his progress. As he pressed forward into a world of emptiness and of deadening silence, dream must have intensified into a nightmare of *déjà vu*. Whatever self-possession he may have had at the outset must long since have drained away when, crossing Wumen, he finally entered the precinct of the Forbidden City."[3]

Fortress-like Wumen is a gate-house with two wings projecting forward. Over its main hall and the four pavilions at each end of its wings are double-eaved roofs which help to raise the height of the gate to 125 feet from the ground, making it the tallest structure in the Forbidden City. Government offices once occupied the pavilions. And it was from this gate, every winter, that the new calendar from the president of the Board of Astronomy was proclaimed to the populace.

During the Ming dynasty, the emperor sat high on this bastion to deliver judgment on the prisoners of war captured by his troops. The captives knelt in chains on the granite flagstones below. After their charges were read out, a petition for their execution in the marketplace was presented with due solemnity by the minister of justice. "The reply from the throne — 'Take them there; be it so ordered' — could not have been heard by all present. The order, however, was repeated by the two nobles standing immedi-ately next to the sovereign and then echoed in succession by four, eight, sixteen and thirty-two guardsmen, until it touched off a thundering shout of the same order by the entire battalion of soldiers, their chests inflated."[4]

Three vaulted openings pierce the wall of the Meridian Gate. On the rare occasions that the emperor left the Forbidden City, he departed from the central archway, and likewise passed through it when he re-entered the Palace. Two exceptions to this

Square in front of the Gate of Supreme Harmony.

exclusive practice were made: the empress was allowed to enter the Palace by the central opening on her wedding day; and the top three candidates of the imperial examina-tions, held triennially in Beijing, processed in triumph out of it after their results were announced.

Let us follow our imaginary visitor as he emerges from the dark archway under Wumen into the bright spacious courtyard

平定回部
獻俘
閫首霍占
末月竄傾
心末坦欵
天閤理官
淋詢寧
頂試驟騎
竄近賓奇
臧西海永
清武保定
午門三御
典昭詳医
今更頃冬
斯事体養
吾民共樂
康辰吞妻
月上游作
御章

beyond. He has arrived at the Outer Court, where the official business of the empire is conducted. We see that this open square is cut by a bow-shaped stream, straddled in its middle stretch by five arched bridges. To the north, the double-eaved Gate of Supreme Harmony (Taihemen) stands on a terrace. As he comes in sight of it, the visitor, if he is a civil official, would make for the opening on the eastern side, the one called the Gate of

Luminous Virtue (Zhaodemen). Military men used the doorway opposite, the Gate of Correct Conduct (Zhengdumen). The central one was reserved for the emperor.

Stepping through, the official allows his gaze to fall upon the white marble balustrades ahead and sweep upward to the glowing golden roofs of the Hall of Supreme Harmony. It lingers on the curious figures on the sloping ridges, although they are not curious

Captives taken in battle being presented at Meridian Gate.

to *him*, of course, since he knows they have been put there to guard the building against fire. Still, those gaping dragons, phoenixes, flying horses and other mythical beasts, in silhouette against the sky, can only add to his sense of being in a dream. Across the huge barren courtyard, the three-tiered marble terrace on which the Hall of Supreme Harmony stands is climbed by wide flights of stairs. There is no question but that the official's progress is one of ascent in the symbolic sense as well, for he is approaching the very center of imperial power.

The most important rituals of an emperor's ceremonial life were enacted in the Hall of Supreme Harmony — enthronement, New Year celebrations and receiving formal felicitations on his birthday. More often than not, the emperor, high on his throne, could not be seen by his kowtowing subjects at all, being concealed behind a haze of smoke thrown up by the sandalwood and pine smoldering in the incense burners below.

We shall leave our official here, and proceed on our tour toward the buildings immediately behind. With the Hall of Supreme Harmony, two other buildings sharing the foundation of the marble terrace make up the group known as the Three Front Halls. These are the Hall of Central Harmony (Zhonghedian), a sort of anteroom to the main audience hall, where the start of the agricultural year was marked by a ritual inspection of plows and seeds; and the Hall of Preserving Harmony (Baohedian), a reception room for envoys, ambassadors and scholars who had achieved the most distinguished results in the civil service examinations. The Hall of

Central Harmony is the smallest of the three, square in plan, and surmounted by a single-hipped roof, its four sloping ridges gathered up into a gilded spherical finial. The third building, the Hall of Preserving Harmony, is similar to the Hall of Supreme Harmony but

The Ming emperor Jiajing (reigned 1522-66).

smaller and less grandiose. Reflecting its lower ranking in the scale of importance, it has a double-eaved but half-hipped roof.

To the east and west of the central trio of halls are other groups of buildings, some of them set around courtyards, others arranged in rows. They served a variety of purposes, now all but forgotten. Many of them were

doubtless storehouses, offices or archives. The Grand Secretariat had its quarters east of the Meridian Gate, and a well for the imperial kitchen was located on the same side. During the Qing dynasty, the Imperial Household Department (Neiwufu), which looked after the emperor's personal property including land, bullion and other palaces, had offices to the west of the Hall of Central Harmony, and the Treasury was in front of it.

Beyond the Three Front Halls, and covering less than half of the total space of the Forbidden City, lie the domestic quarters of the Palace. Known as the Inner Court, this part of the Palace will be explored in another chapter. Suffice it to say now that there, too, is the symmetrical arrangement of halls and spaces, the same painted beams and brackets, the contrast of white marble and red walls. The beauty of the Forbidden City owes as much to this unity of style as to the architecture of the buildings themselves — the whole is indeed immensely greater than the sum of its parts.

1   Wan-Go Weng and Yang Boda: *The Palace Museum: Peking*

2   L.C. Arlington and William Lewisohn: *In Search of Old Peking*

3   William Willets: *Foundations of Chinese Art*

4   Ray Huang: *1587: A Year of No Significance*

SON OF HEAVEN

The sovereign of the Chinese empire assumed on his accession a role of breathtaking complexity. He had to be commander of the army and enlightened statesman, moral leader and hierarch, legislator and supreme judge, patron of learning and chief examiner, administrator and bureaucrat.

How was this complex role manifested within the Forbidden City? In this and the following chapters, we shall look to several emperors — particularly Wanli (reigned 1573-1620), Kangxi (reigned 1662-1722) and Qianlong (reigned 1736-95) — to give us a glimpse of what was involved.

The emperor Yongle, who usurped the throne from his nephew and built the capital city of Beijing, inherited a highly autocratic form of government. Its pyramidal structure began with the smallest local unit, the county, presided over by a magistrate whose chief responsibilities were the collection of land taxes, the maintenance of law and order, and the selection of scholars for the civil service examinations. The next level was the prefecture, and several prefectures formed a province. A province was a very large area indeed, and each one was controlled by a governor, who was in turn in the charge of a grand coordinator. The civil system was

mirrored by a military one — the chain of responsibility led from local guard garrisons to regional military commissions, regional commanders and a supreme commander —

(Opposite) Throne in the Hall of Supreme Harmony. (Above) Badge of a military official of the first grade.

---

although the military corps was never as politically important as the civil.

In the central government, the principal organs of state were five chief military commissions, six ministries or boards and the traditional censorate. Since the office of prime minister was abolished by Yongle's father, executive power had become increasingly concentrated in the emperor's hands. For advice and assistance he would turn to the Grand Secretariat, a body of scholars instituted by the first Ming emperor in 1380.

Though intended to be chiefly concerned with putting imperial decisions into suitable prose for edicts, rather than with implementing policy, nevertheless the Grand Secretariat gradually extended its influence over the six boards and acquired authority over the whole bureaucracy. All officials were, however, subject to the supervision of the censorate, a surveillance body whose function — at least in theory — was to root out cases of corruption and malpractice and to keep the whole system working smoothly and effectively.

A large bureaucracy managed the enormous flow of memorials and edicts that passed between local and provincial authorities and the central government. Reports and petitions to the throne might be initiated by governors wishing to raise issues or to suggest solutions to problems; decisions taken after due consideration of these memorials would then be handed down in the form of rescripts or edicts drafted by the Grand Secretariat.

As with all bureaucracies, the Chinese civil service was adept at generating too much paper, but perhaps only thirty to fifty documents reached the emperor on a normal working day. They were generally submitted by officials reporting or requesting decisions on public matters and dealt with routinely;

occasionally they were memorials of a more personal nature, requiring the emperor's comment. Written on long rolls of paper folded four, eight or more times concertina-like into compact, manageable sizes, they would be annotated by the emperor in red ink with a simple "Acknowledged" or "Approved," or a more detailed message.

The vermilion ink was a mark of the emperor's authority, affirmed on an almost daily basis. But imperial authority was even more powerfully expressed in the grand ceremonial audience. This stood out from the regular court audiences, which punctu-ated the imperial calendar of duties, by its splendor and panoply. No government business was in fact carried out at a grand audience; its sole purpose was to demonstrate the power and glory of the Son of Heaven. It would not have mattered if the emperor was personally absent, as he sometimes was. The homage would then simply be paid to an empty throne.

The grand audience was held for such events as enthronement, marriage and to mark the New Year. During the Qing

Display of insignia at emperor Guangxu's wedding celebrations.

dynasty, audiences were also arranged in the Hall of Supreme Harmony on the fifth, fifteenth and twenty-fifth of each lunar month. Their function too was merely formal: officials and military governors would come, for instance, to take leave of their sovereign before departing for their provin-cial postings, to express their gratitude for favors granted or to pay their respects on receiving a promotion. Emperor Kangxi considered audiences an institution of great significance. "A court audience has the important function of reducing arrogance. Of course one can't summon all military governors for audiences at the same time, but regular audiences are crucial with military men, especially when they have held power a long time."[1] There was nothing like the act of prostration to remind a man of his inferiority.

We can reconstruct the scene of a grand audience from the series of paintings executed to record the wedding in 1889 of the emperor Guangxu (reigned 1875-1908). At the ceremony, held three days after the nuptials, the proclamation of his marriage would be made from the Gate of Heavenly Peace, and felicitations from his nobles and officials would be formally accepted.

The square in front of the Hall of Supreme Harmony, the triple flights of marble stairs, the wide terrace at the top, had been cleared, swept and decorated. A length of carpet stretched across the great square. Courtiers started arriving before dawn, their way into the Forbidden City lit by lanterns. Peals of ritual music greeted them as they hurried through the gates — on foot, of course, for they could only ride or be carried in a palanquin if they were very old and frail, or by special imperial dispensation.

Inside, the courtiers took their positions according to rank. Atop the terrace and upon the steps were the princes and Manchu

nobility. Below in the huge square — large enough to accommodate twenty thousand men if the need arose — the officials of the nine grades were spread out on the cold flagstones. They were lined up in double rows, with the civil officials on the east and

An official in front of the Forbidden City, by Zhu Bang.

the military commanders on the west. Civil officials traditionally enjoyed a higher status than military commanders, and in the hierar-

chy of the cardinal points east was more esteemed than west. Each official knew his appointed station, since there were bronze-capped markers on the flagstones, in the shape of miniature mountains, to guide him.

In the dim light cast by flickering lanterns, the assembled officials shivered, for it was the first lunar month of the year, and the sun was not yet up to warm them as they waited. Censors moved among them, taking the roll and noting an askew hat here or an over-loud snatch of conversation there. For showing such lack of respect the perpetrators would have their salaries docked afterward.

Did they have eyes for the imposing hall, the arrangements of pillars and beams that supported the hipped roofs with their swooping eaves, or the ornamental brackets painted in patterns of blue, green and white? Spectacular though the vista was, it was unlikely that they felt anything but awe. And, on that day, the massed insignia carried by the honor guard — all those embroidered pennons, dragon-emblazoned parasols and multicolored shields — were dazzling enough.

A hush fell as a whip was raised in the distance to call the ceremony to order. At the sound of cracking, the master of ceremonies shouted "*Kou shou!*" ["Kowtow!"] His

Emperor Kangxi patronized scholarship and worked hard at his calligraphy. As a young man he was tutored in the Confucian classics.

command was echoed by others stationed on the steps and down the length of the square. From under the eaves of the hall, singers chanted and an orchestra played. A fluttering of peacock feathers on mandarin hats, an exaggerated shaking of long silken sleeves, and the entire assembly dropped onto its knees. As they performed their triple kowtow — three prostrations and nine knockings of the forehead on the hard flagstones — the officials might have strained their eyes to see beyond the insignia, the guards, the representatives from the Board of Rites and the princes of the blood. But the emperor, sitting on his elevated golden throne, flanked by gilded pillars decorated with coiling dragons, guarded by a bevy of his "leopard-tail" troop and screened by columns of wavering smoke from incense burners, was as remote, untouchable and mysterious as the moon. Like an icon, he had been carried in his yellow satin chair to the place of worship, and would be whisked away before his acolytes could catch more than a fleeting glimpse of him. Music of great antiquity accompanied his arrival and departure.

More rites were to follow. An official announcement of the nuptials had to be communicated to the emperor's subjects. This demanded an elaborate procedure, similar to the proclamation of imperial edicts. First the announcement in the form of a scroll was carried on a gilded tray through the Meridian Gate to a waiting sedan chair, a "dragon pavilion" *(longting)*. Ensconced in the dragon pavilion, the announcement was conveyed in state to the Gate of Heavenly Peace, where it was retrieved by waiting officials, taken to the top of the gate and read out. Then the scroll was ceremoniously lowered in its tray by a cord threaded

Carved marble ramp on the stairway behind the Hall of Preserving Harmony.

through the beak of a gilded phoenix. (So were edicts graciously bestowed on the populace, though they descended to a kneeling official, tray in hand, not in a sling but in the beak of a bronze crane.) Finally, the scroll was returned to the Palace in the dragon pavilion. All was pure theater, and such was the power of these pageants to inspire awe and obedience that the staging of rituals was practically the most important function of the court. One of the six ministries in the central government, the Board of Rites, devoted itself to the arrangements.

The four offices of the Board of Rites were responsible for court ceremonies, sacrifices, the reception of foreign envoys and tributary affairs, and banquets. Organizing ceremonies naturally involved attending to formal clothes, regalia, music and other related matters, but the Board of Rites also directed education and the conduct of the imperial examinations which selected able men for public service.

The Chinese left more literature about the theory and practice of government than most other civilizations. They believed that their venerated philosopher Confucius (551–479 BC) had developed the perfect political and social system in which man was civilized by education and discipline to pursue purposes that were truly virtuous. According to Confucius, "Only by perfect virtue can the perfect path, in all its courses, be made a fact."[2] Virtue was the mainspring of society's well-being, and the linchpin of the whole system was the personal character of the ruler. When asked about government, Confucius had replied, "To govern means to rectify. If you lead on the people with correctness, who will dare not to be correct . . . Let your evinced desires be for what is good, and the people will be good. The relation between superiors and inferiors is like that between the wind and the grass. The grass must bend, when the wind blows across it."

"It is only he, possessed of all sagely qualities that can exist under heaven, who

shows himself quick in apprehension, clear in discernment, of far-reaching intelligence, and all-embracing knowledge, fitted to exercise rule . . ." Only if the ruler demonstrated sagely qualities would he merit the mandate to rule, a mandate sanctioned by the gods and ancestors on high whom the Chinese called by the collective name "Heaven." Indeed, such a ruler would be "the equal of Heaven" or "the Son of Heaven."

As the recipient of the divine mandate, therefore, the emperor was expected to conform to the Confucian model in a tangible way. "Hence the sovereign may not neglect the cultivation of his own character," said Confucius, since " . . . the superior man

honours his virtuous nature, and maintains constant inquiry and study, seeking to carry it out to its breadth and greatness . . ." The emperor had to be seen to be striving toward the ideal through constant attention to self-education. His role as ruler was thus inter-twined with that of scholar: as the supreme scholar of the realm he personally endorsed the results of the *dianshi,* the triennial imperial examinations, by granting an audience to the successful candidates and allowing the best scholars to leave the Palace through the central archway of the Meridian Gate.

We are, once again, at the great bastion that guards the entrance to the Palace. We also leave the Forbidden City at this point,

Ming-dynasty painting of imperial examination candidates awaiting their results.

---

but we shall be accompanying the emperor and his retinue, not the triumphant scholars, through the Meridian Gate. It is the winter solstice, time for the emperor to pray and offer sacrifice to his ancestors and to Heaven.

1   Jonathan D. Spence: *Emperor of China: Self-Portrait of K'ang-hsi*
2   The quotations of Confucius are from "The Doctrine of the Mean," in *Confucius,* translated by James Legge

DRAGONS AND CRANES
SYMBOLS OF OFFICE

First there was the color — bright yellow. Striking enough, but it was chosen for a purpose. The yellow of an emperor's formal robe represented earth, a source of nourishment and life. Then there were the twelve imperial motifs, painstakingly woven or embroidered with threads of gold, red, blue, green and white, over months and years, by the many nimble needleworkers of Suzhou or Hangzhou. These motifs, too, had a cosmic significance. Central to them was the five-clawed dragon, the highest and most powerful of all animals, and identified with the emperor since ancient times. It decorated not only his clothes; it crawled up the pillars of his Palace, it embellished the utensils on his table, it was carved in jade on his seal. On his court dress, dragons were placed across the chest, on the back, shoulders, collar, cuffs and the skirt, and along the button flap. Above them floated the clouds, a symbol for Heaven, and below them were the beautiful diagonal striations of swirling waves and foaming breakers, parted in places by mountain peaks; these of course denoted the oceans and the earth. The highest of all animals was complemented by the highest of all avians, the pheasant. Add the symbols for the sun, the moon and the stars, and we have the entire universe.

Other symbols of imperial authority were scattered on the fabric — a stylized Chinese character *(fu)* and an axe represented temporal power; sacrificial goblets, a water plant, a plate of millet and tongues of flame stood for the elements — metal, water, wood and fire.

The dragon robes which survive in museums date from the Qing dynasty. It is thought that the cut of the garment — a fitted jacket over a loose pleated skirt — can be traced to the Manchus' riding costume, but we know that the motifs were traditionally Chinese. This is also true of the symbols on *buzi,* or "mandarin squares" as they are termed by collectors, sewn onto an official's coat. Known as rank insignia, the symbols in the form of embroidered birds or animals were introduced in the Ming dynasty and later adopted by the Qing rulers.

The Qing officials who came to audiences with the emperor in the square of the Hall of Supreme Harmony knew where to stand, for the bronze markers on the flagstones indicated their positions in order of rank. On their person, too, the exact rung of the bureaucratic and military ladders to which they belonged was easily distinguishable, being emblazoned across their black or dark blue coats. In the civil corps, the crane represented the first grade, the golden pheasant the second grade, then the peacock, the wild goose, the silver pheasant, the egret, the mandarin duck, the quail and the paradise flycatcher down to the ninth grade. Military badges sported first the *qilin*, a mythical animal like a unicorn, followed by the lion, the leopard, the tiger, the bear, the tiger cat, the rhinoceros (worn by officials of both the seventh and eighth grades) and the sea horse. The bird or animal was either woven or embroidered against a multicolored background filled with symbols such as clouds, the sun or the moon and bats. But nothing was random, neither the pattern nor the colors. Every detail, like that on a dragon robe, conformed to what was deemed proper, auspicious and conducive to harmony and prosperity.

MANDATE OF HEAVEN

Ten days before the winter solstice, the Palace would start its preparations for the annual sacrifice to Heaven, an event of paramount importance in the imperial calendar. It was approaching the time of year when the sun, if it could be seen, appeared to stand still, and the raw, dry winds from the Mongolian desert sent the temperatures plummeting. Everyone knew that *yin* was approaching its nadir and *yang* was beginning to return to ascendancy, for that was how, according to the ancient dualist principle, the negative and positive forces interacted to transform the universe.

A list of the names of all those intending to take part in the ceremony was submitted to the Court of Sacrificial Worship. Each man, in his heart, reviewed the rules of ritual purification. In the three days before the sacrifice, no banquets could be held nor music played. Participants had to abstain from sexual intercourse, renounce alcohol and certain foods, and keep their distance from the sick and the bereaved. Spitting was to be avoided at all cost — a not inconsiderable deprivation in Beijing's dry climate. Judicial procedures would be suspended, and the sweeping of graves was taboo. Lest they

forget, some of the participants would hang a tablet round their necks to remind them to be vigilant. The emperor, no less than the others, observed the strict rules of purification; and to help *him* remember, a bronze

(Opposite) The Hall of Prayer for Good Harvests. (Above) Three tiers of marble enclosed by carved balustrades make up the Round Mound.

statue holding a board, inscribed with a gentle admonition to refrain from self-indulgence, was placed in the Hall of Abstinence.

For two days and nights the emperor kept vigil in the Hall of Abstinence in the Forbidden City. On the eve of the appointed day, he was dressed in a dragon robe and carried in a sedan chair from the Inner Court to the stairs below the Gate of Supreme Harmony. There he was set down and escorted to his

jade carriage, and it was in this curtained and jade-embellished conveyance that he would travel to the Temple of Heaven four miles south of the Forbidden City. Outside the Meridian Gate, princes, nobles, officials and commanders, formally attired in their court robes, waited on their knees for the imperial procession to pass. (When the emperor returned the next day, they would be there, again on their knees, to welcome him back.)

It was a splendid procession. Since this was classified as one of the Three Great Sacrifices, the worship of Heaven demanded a full-scale deployment of the honor guard, the imperial insignia and the countless attendants and eunuchs involved in transporting the ritual objects necessary to the ceremony. In the winter of 1784 it was the emperor Qianlong who performed the annual sacrifice. His entourage included 660 guards, some carrying swords, others bows and arrows. There were senior officials on horseback, musicians on foot and elephant-drawn carriages. Hundreds of pennants and banners flapped in the wind as the 3,700-strong retinue wended its way from the Forbidden City southward to the Temple of Heaven. As they marched, the only sounds were the creak of the car-

riages, the tinkling of bells, the ponderous thud of elephants' feet and the soft whinnying of the short-necked ponies that the officials rode, for they traveled on a route previously sprinkled with yellow sand. No prying eyes marked their majestic progress, the citizens having been warned beforehand to keep indoors or risk a severe lashing.

To reach the Temple of Heaven the entourage passed through the great gateway of the Inner City, Qianmen, and down the thoroughfare which, straight as an arrow, delineated the north-south axis of the city. Soon the signs of the city were left behind, and the worshipers came to the road, branching off to their left, that would take them into the precincts of the holiest site in China. In European architecture, cathedrals with their high domes, vaulted naves and arched windows, all suggesting a reaching-up to

Heaven, were built to create interior spaces. Worshipers at the Temple of Heaven were surrounded by devices that emphasized the same aspiration — of the shrine being a bridge between the earthbound and the celestial — but here the huge altar was set in an exterior space and bare under the sky. It was enclosed only by groves of trees. The somber cypresses, with their distinctive summer foliage of dark silvery green, were planted by emperor Jiajing in 1530.

The two supremely lovely structures at the Temple of Heaven are this open altar (known as the Round Mound) and the Hall of Prayer for Good Harvests. Few religious sites can boast a shrine reflecting such purity of conception as the Round Mound, a simple and magnificent design consisting of three ascending tiers of white marble, with three sets of balustrades. Above the balus-

(Above) Sacrifice at the Temple of Agriculture by the emperor Yongzheng. (Page 43) Equatorial armillary on a dragon-decorated bronze stand, made by Verbiest for the emperor Kangxi.

trades rise 360 balusters carved with dragons, phoenixes and clouds, the number of balusters on each tier being in multiples of nine, the most auspicious and ultimate *yang* numeral. Like the architectural elements of the Forbidden City, the Round Mound and ancillary structures are suffused with cosmological symbolism. The first set of walls that encloses the open altar (and indeed the altar itself) is round, round as the blue dome of the sky, while the outer wall is square and representative of the earth. The exact locations of the archways; the specific numbers of tiers, balustrades and paving stones of the altar; the compass directions faced by the shrines to secondary deities that would share the oblations at the winter solstice sacrifice — all were rigidly prescribed and charged with symbolic meaning. Also raised on three tiers of marble, the Hall of Prayer for Good Harvests is crowned by a triple-eaved conical roof, brilliant with sapphire blue tiles and tapering to a gilded ball — a glittering jewel silhouetted against the pale winter sky. For many a spectator, the whole temple complex offers a vision of abstract and austere beauty.

Perhaps emperor Qianlong, entering the temple grounds from the west gate, stopped and admired. If so, he might have contemplated the prospect with some satisfaction, since it was he who in 1749 ordered the altar to be rebuilt with that white stone and the roof of the hall to be refaced with those gleaming tiles. Then he alighted from his carriage, his attention quickly claimed by the duties that awaited him. He must now make his way to the Imperial Vault of Heaven, where he would offer incense to his ancestors and perform the triple kowtow. Afterward, catching the last light of the day, he would inspect the preparations at the circular altar, now decked out with silk tents in a deep shade of blue. The shrine to the supreme deity of Heaven, Shangdi, was placed under its blue canopy north of the center of the top tier. It was flanked by shrines to former emperors, and, on the middle tier, to the secondary gods of the sun, the moon, the stars, and the clouds, rain, wind and thunder.

The only formal occasion when the emperor turned his back to the south would be the next day, when he would fall on his knees in front of Shangdi's shrine.

As twilight descended, Qianlong retired to observe his last day of fast in the temple's own Hall of Abstinence. His father Yongzheng (reigned 1723-35) had inaugurated the custom of dividing the three days' ritual purification between the Forbidden City and the Temple of Heaven. Qianlong, if he gave it any thought, could only have been glad that the heated chamber where he was to spend the night was no less comfortable than his room in the Palace.

Lanterns burned through the night. In the sacred abattoir at the eastern corner of the temple enclosure, a bullcalf, a sheep, a pig and a deer were killed in a solemn ceremony, amid offerings of prayers and incense, and then carried down a long candle-lit corridor to the sacrificial furnace.

Qianlong woke three hours after midnight. His final act of purification was a bath. Eunuchs then helped him on with his imperial yellow robe, their faces as still and impassive as a bottomless pool. The emperor too was holding his energies in reserve for the great moment that was to come. His eyes fell briefly on the arcane motifs of his gown, rich with meaning. They hinted at his place in the universal scheme of things: Son of Heaven, high priest and intercessor for his people. Running his hand over the embossed

dragons, he was moved by an overwhelming recognition of his destiny — he felt great issues looming about him, but with that came also an awareness of both strength and pain. His was the heaviest burden a man was ever called upon to bear. He was entrusted with a mandate to rule over the earth, and he alone worshiped Heaven and possessed the authority to make the sacrifices effective. The fortunes of mankind — "all under Heaven" — depended on his pure virtue and moral conduct. At the dawn of the winter solstice, up there on the sacred altar, he would report on how he had acquitted himself during the preceding year. If he had exercised righteous government and performed the religious rites as ordained by past tradition, Heaven would respond with the utmost beneficence, harmony would prevail on earth and his mandate to rule would be affirmed. If he had been corrupt and tyrannical, natural disasters would devastate the land, crops would fail and famine would follow. Too many cycles of floods, drought and famine, and the mandate might be withdrawn, justifying popular rebellion and the overthrow of his dynasty.

The concept of the Mandate of Heaven, like the sacrifice to Shangdi, dated back to the early beginnings of Chinese history. Qianlong, preparing to leave the Hall of Abstinence, must have felt the past, present and future fusing together in that moment of exquisite anticipation, minutes away from his communion with Heaven, when his mandate would once again be renewed. Through the year he had attended, or sent the princes and officials to attend on his behalf, a seemingly incessant cycle of rites to ensure harmony and the continuance of his dynasty. There was the worship at the Temple of Agriculture in the spring, where he himself had plowed three furrows, the Altar of the Earth, the Altar of the Sun and the Altar of the Moon, not to mention the devotions offered at the Altar of the Land and Grain, the shrine to Confucius and the Temple of the Imperial Ancestors. Elaborate or simple, those ceremonies absorbed thirty to forty days of the year, involving an unremitting round of purification and sacrifices. They had been properly conducted, though, for no portents or inauspicious signs had appeared to disturb the realm, and the empire enjoyed peace and prosperity.

At four o'clock, one hour and forty-five minutes before sunrise, to the accompaniment of a tolling bell, the imperial carriage conveyed the emperor along paths bordered by leafless trees to the pavilion where he changed his clothes for the appropriate sacrificial robe. Heat from an underground flue warmed the pavilion where he dressed. Meanwhile the spirit tablets of Shangdi and the imperial ancestors were reverently brought to the Round Mound and placed in the shrines, where individual altar tables were already laden with offerings of wine, meats, grains and silk.

All the other participants had taken their assigned places on the lowest tier of the Round Mound and at the sides. These included musicians, singers and dancers, and at each stage of the ceremony, they would play or chant or posture in accordance with rules and procedures established by the Board of Rites long ago.

The ceremony was in three parts, and each part included three separate acts. A roll of drums and music signaled the beginning of the first service. The Son of Heaven mounted the Round Mound, accompanied by two directors of the rites, one of whom would prompt him on the acts he was to perform. On the topmost tier of the altar, the emperor offered incense first to Shangdi, then in turn to the ancestors. The offering completed, he withdrew to the middle tier, where he prostrated himself in the triple kowtow. Next, the emperor made his first libation, and this was followed by the reading of the prayer. While the official reader intoned it, the emperor knelt on his yellow cushion in a pose of humble reverence. Thereafter, for the rest of the service, he went through more or less the same motions, with offerings of jade, silk and victuals. The ceremony climaxed in a final symbolic act of spiritual union, when the emperor himself drank the wine and partook of the meat.

Although dawn was almost breaking, it was still freezing, and the icy air stung his throat, but coughing was forbidden, so Qianlong held his breath. Opaque shadows hovered in the eerie light of torches. When his forehead touched the cold hard stone, for the thirty-sixth time that night, the Son of Heaven felt again that strength and pain, but experienced as well a curious sense of triumph. He was the anointed instrument, the only earthly representative able to carry out the will of Heaven; he had in him the power to conciliate the forces of nature. Hadn't the Master said: "To no one but the Son of Heaven does it belong to order ceremonies . . . One may occupy the throne, but if he have not the proper virtue, he may not dare to make ceremonies or music"?[1] This morning, he had indeed ordered ceremonies and music, and the sacrifices *would* be effective.

A ghostly tune assailed his ears: the spirit tablets were being removed to the accompaniment of the music "Pure Peace." He prostrated himself once more. After the final kowtow, the participants dispersed in the direction of the sacrificial furnace, where a fire of pine and cypress logs already filled the air with a smoky fragrance. There, watched over by the emperor, the prayer, the silk and the offerings of wine, meats and grains were consigned to the flames.

1 Confucius: "The Doctrine of the Mean," in *Confucius*, translated by James Legge

On May 16, 1585, the fourteenth Ming emperor, a descendant of Yongle, went to the Temple of Heaven to pray for rain. The Wanli emperor was deeply worried: the drought that had started the previous year showed no signs of breaking, causing much hardship among his subjects. It was clear to him that the celestial harmony had been disturbed. Such a calamity, he reasoned, reflected his own shortcomings as ruler, although he blamed the officials as well: their ineffectiveness, despite much fervent praying, had also clearly offended Heaven.

On this occasion, the usual pomp and circumstance would be dispensed with; the situation was far too grave for anything but the most simple and solemn proceedings. As a further sign of his earnestness, Wanli decided that he and the whole party would ride neither horse nor carriage, but go to the Temple of Heaven on foot. And after the sacrifice, though the imperial carriage had been ordered by his attendant eunuchs, Wanli refused it and walked all the way back again to the Forbidden City, obliging his officials to do the same.

It had been a dreadfully hot and exhausting day. But Wanli's intercession with Heaven was apparently successful, though he had to wait nearly a month for the rains to come.

Drought and floods are terrible scourges for an agrarian people. But the emperor's special relationship with Heaven was supposed to protect the farmer from such calamities. A philosopher wrote in around 100 BC: "If the ruler is correct, then the creative energies will be harmonious and compliant, winds and rain will be timely, auspicious stars will appear, and the yellow dragon will descend." When everything was in harmonious balance, night would follow day, spring would follow winter and the right times to sow and reap would be manifest. To the simple farmer, knowing when to expect rain and sun could be a matter of life and death. The earliest Chinese emperors took it upon themselves to provide a guide and employed astronomers to compile calendars, the accuracy of which became associated with imperial prestige. In fact, calendar-making was of such political importance that the observatory was controlled by the central government and the imperial astronomer held one of the highest-ranking offices in the capital.

In time the official almanac became also a source of astrological information. As well as concerning itself with such matters as the prediction of solar and lunar eclipses, it interpreted the movements

of celestial bodies in terms of human affairs and made prophecies of good and bad fortune. Thus the calendar not only named the times for plowing, sowing and harvesting, it also specified the favorable days for such actions of everyday life as getting married, moving house, sweeping graves or undertaking a journey.

It was the tradition for a new calendar to be published by the Imperial Calendrical Bureau (later the Board of Astronomy) in the eleventh lunar month and ceremoniously bestowed on a grateful populace. This required the presence of the imperial astronomer, who personally took the yellow bound volumes to the Meridian Gate. There, a special sedan chair waited to convey the emperor's copy to him in the Inner Court. Meanwhile, civil and military officials carried the new calendar to the Gate of Heavenly Peace, where it was formally proclaimed to the people.

The Chinese used the visible phases of the moon to measure

time. But the seasons of the year are governed by the orbit of the earth around the sun. Twelve lunar months fall several days short of a complete cycle of the seasons, so that every few years it becomes necessary to insert an extra or intercalary month if the seasons are to come round always in the same numbered month. This was rather complicated and confounded the Chinese court astronomers; their calendars became less and less exact, and their predictions of the solar eclipse frequently proved wrong. Help came in the form of a "barbarian," a Jesuit missionary, followed by his brothers, who demonstrated how to measure accurately days, months and the rhythm of the seasons. Not only that, they had even more sophisticated methods of marking the passage of time — they brought the mechanical clock.

(Opposite) Clock, made in England, in the collection of the Palace Museum. (Left) A flotilla of barges with the emperor Wanli in the center. (Above) Another astronomical instrument made by Verbiest, a silver-gilt armillary sphere.

Barbarians at the Forbidden City

In September 1583 the Jesuit priest Matteo Ricci landed in southern China. He had spent an enforced two-year sojourn in the Portuguese colony of Macao, which had been chosen by the Holy See as its base for converting the people of the Far East to the Christian faith. There Ricci had waited for a summons to the mainland, the real objective of Rome's missionary ambitions. During the two years, Ricci had acquired an elementary command of Mandarin, the Beijing dialect of the north, rather than Cantonese, the dialect spoken in Macao. He chose Mandarin as it was the language of the officials; his goal was to penetrate the Forbidden City, for he had quickly realized that to convert any souls he had first to convince the officials as well as Wanli, the emperor of the time, of the benefits of Christianity.

Ricci and his traveling companion Father Ruggieri arrived in Zhaoqing at the invitation of the local governor, who had heard tell of their mastery in mathematics. The governor gave them a small piece of land on which to build their mission house and urged them "to become in all but physical appearance, men of the Middle Kingdom, subject to the Emperor."[1] Heeding this advice, they took to wearing the Chinese outer garment, a long robe with ample sleeves, which resembled the fathers' own religious habit.

An extraordinarily talented linguist — he could soon boast five thousand Chinese characters — a scientist, geographer and mathematician, Ricci quickly assimilated himself into Chinese society. But, although

(Opposite) The Catholic Church, Beitang — Kangxi first granted the Jesuits permission to build a church on this site. (Above) Matteo Ricci.

there were frequent visitors to the mission house, the fathers well knew that the interest they aroused in the local community was because of their learning and in particular of Ricci's memory. He would ask a visitor to inscribe five hundred characters, then with one look he would recite them back.

It was a tortuous eighteen years before Ricci gained permission to go to Beijing, by which time the Mandate of Heaven was beginning to slip from the Ming dynasty's grasp. Emperor Wanli's concern for his subjects' welfare, so conscientiously expressed in his prayer for rain, had given way to indifference. Ensconced in the Great Within, he had long stopped holding audiences and simply withdrawn from public view.

The experience of those waiting years had taught Ricci to appreciate China's intellectual tradition and the importance of the Confucian classics in Chinese society. He realized that to be successful it was necessary for him to try to understand how the Chinese thought, and he consciously began to interpret any Confucian ambiguities in a Catholic light. The fathers discarded the robes of Buddhist monks, which they had adopted, for those of the revered literati: purple silk, a border of light blue around the neck, topped off with a tall black hat.

On May 18, 1600 Ricci and another priest, Father Didaco Pantoia, supervised the packing of their personal belongings on board a barge, part of a flotilla bound up the Grand Canal carrying a cargo of silk to Beijing. They stowed "enough furniture for a new house and for a fully equipped chapel," and a selection of gifts for the emperor including a large clock, "set in its enclosure with four columns. The case was built with folding doors, opening on either side. The hours were marked on the face of the clock in Chinese capital letters, with an eagle dominating, which pointed to the hour with its beak . . . It was an ornament that might well have been placed on exhibition in Europe."[2]

An eventful journey followed. In Tianjin the fathers were imprisoned by the eunuch official Ma Tang, a corrupt tax collector. The eunuch originally offered to help, claiming he had enough influence at court to gain the fathers an audience with the emperor, but later he grew suspicious and placed them under house arrest. In the end his assistance was not needed at all. Divine Providence came to the fathers' aid, for it was the emperor himself who sanctioned their onward journey. "The Emperor Wanli inquired one day, 'where is the clock, I say, where is that clock which rings of itself: the one the foreigners were bringing here to me, as they said in their petition?' 'Your Majesty', came the reply, 'if you have not as yet sent an answer to the letter of the eunuch Mathan [Ma Tang], how could the foreigners have entered the royal city without your permission?"[3] So, after travels lasting eight months, the party finally entered Beijing on January 24, 1601; the next day the presents were paraded across town to the Palace.

Ricci's petition to Wanli had been in the manner of a vassal bearing tribute — a further indication of his readiness to adopt the supplicant style conventional in memorials to the emperor. Using his Chinese name Li Madou, he said that he had come from the Far West and respectfully begged permission to present His Majesty with some presents, of a kind which had not heretofore been seen in China. Apart from the large clock there was another smaller one, a clavichord, some religious pictures, crucifixes and relics (deemed by the suspicious Board of Rites "bones of Immortals, as if Immortals did not take their bones with them to Heaven!"[4]). As for qualifications, he continued, he thoroughly understood the celestial sphere, geography and geometry and mathematics. He could make calculations with the astrolabe and the gnomon by methods, he said, which were in accordance with Chinese precedent. If the emperor Wanli would deign to accept the services of so inconsiderable a scholar, his endeavors would only be exceeded by his happiness in working for the Sovereign Lord of the World.

When the summons from the Forbidden City came, it was because one of the clocks had stopped. It must have struck Ricci as bizarre that, after eighteen years of dogged struggle, it was the palace eunuchs' need to understand how to wind up a clock that finally gained him the emperor's attention. Indeed the clocks proved to be the Jesuits'

passports. The emperor, fascinated by the clocks, appointed four eunuchs from the Imperial College of Mathematicians to learn from Ricci the skills of clock-keeping. For three days Ricci was lodged in the Forbidden City while the eunuchs grappled with this new technology. Throughout this time Wanli, via eunuch messengers, asked a stream of questions concerning every aspect of life in Europe. There had been much hostility to the idea of allowing the fathers residence in Beijing; the memorial from the Board of Rites to the emperor suggested they be sent back to Macao. However, the eunuchs appointed to look after the large clock, dismayed at the thought that there would be no one to work it once the Jesuits left, used their considerable influence to thwart the suggestion. The emperor chose to ignore the conflict between these two factions: he simply never answered their memorials. So, though they never received written permission to remain in Beijing, the Jesuits moved into their own house, where they stayed until many years after Ricci's death; technically they were still at the guesthouse awaiting the approved decision of the Board of Rites.

Wanli was apparently also fascinated by the clavichord; he ordered four palace musicians to learn to play it. Father Didaco, whom Ricci with great foresight had insisted become proficient on the instrument, took charge of the eunuchs' instruction. Accom-

panying songs were also required so, as Didaco taught, Ricci composed. The result was eight "Songs for the Clavichord," mostly based on Horatian odes. The songs were so popular in literati circles that a book was compiled in both Latin and Chinese. By now a close rapport between the eunuchs and Ricci had developed and, when the clocks went wrong again, a royal order was issued giving the Jesuits the right to visit the Forbidden City whenever they pleased.

Once established under the emperor's patronage, work in the mission progressed. (In fact, Ricci and Wanli never met. Even Wanli's enormous curiosity about the priest would not allow him to throw off his seclusion to take a glimpse at Ricci: he ordered portraits of the Jesuit to be painted instead.) Ricci served Wanli by regulating the clocks, teaching members of the Imperial College of Mathematicians and revising the calendar. He felt that if he could prove to his hosts that they were wrong in material matters, then they would be more likely to listen to his spiritual counsel. Before he died in 1610 he repeatedly implored the Pope to send a good mathematician or astronomer to the court of China for, as he modestly noted in his diary, his science "was none too advanced." " . . . With the help of certain ephemerides and Portuguese almanacs I sometimes predict eclipses more accurately than the court

Emperor Wanli.

astronomers do . . . if the mathematicians of whom I spoke came here, we could readily translate our tables into Chinese characters and rectify their year. This would . . . open wider the gates of China, and would enable us to live more securely and freely."[5]

Twelve years later the true heir of Matteo Ricci, another remarkable Jesuit by the name of Johann Adam Schall von Bell, arrived at the late Ming court. Schall's special talent was astronomy, which he used to recommend much needed reforms to the Chinese calendar. Like Ricci he was able to parlay his technical abilities and fluency in Chinese into imperial patronage and significant influence at court.

Four years after his arrival in Beijing, Schall published in Chinese a description of the Galilean telescope. Then came a major coup. On June 21, 1626 Schall correctly predicted the time and length of an eclipse; the imperial astronomers were one hour out on the timing, and their estimate of the duration was totally wrong. As a result of this show of scholarship, the Jesuits were invited by imperial edict to correct the calendar, said to have been at fault for 350 years.

Perhaps the eclipse was a portent; with hindsight it might even have been interpreted as a presage of a change of dynasty, for

within a short time of its occurrence the empire was shaken by a rebellion against the increasingly ineffectual government of the Ming. Schall's supreme diplomatic achievement was managing, on the overthrow of the Ming by the Qing in 1644, to switch

Adam Schall.

allegiance and to obtain similar privileges from the new dynasty. Even before the new emperor, young Shunzhi (reigned 1644-61), was formally enthroned, the court was inundated with petitions. Among them was one from Adam Schall, who requested permission to test publicly the accuracy of his calculations for a solar eclipse on September 1. The early Qing rulers adopted the

Chinese view of the world as well as the ideas of Confucianism. It did not take them long to realize that the production of an accurate calendar was a vital means of legitimizing their regime.

On the appointed day, Schall took the telescopes and other instruments to the imperial observatory. The Chinese report of the occasion recorded that while the Jesuit's predictions coincided exactly with the timing and location of the eclipse, traditional calculations were wide of the mark. It was a moment of truth too striking to be ignored: the Qing courtiers knew better than to put their new dynasty at risk by issuing calendars inferior to those compiled under the Ming. So they awarded Adam Schall the directorship of the Board of Astronomy, an office of the fifth grade, midway up the ranks of the Chinese bureaucracy.

Schall, however, could not avoid arousing the jealousy of Chinese astronomers, especially that of one Yang Guangxian. Following the death of emperor Shunzhi, Schall was imprisoned on a false charge. In 1666 he and his fellow fathers were released, but by this time Schall was a broken man, and he died that same year in the Jesuit church (Nantang) on the Feast of Assumption.

On Schall's imprisonment the astronomer Yang Guangxian had taken over his official post as well as his house and library of one thousand books. Apparently the books did not improve Yang's calculations, which were frequently inaccurate. This gave Schall's assistant, Father Ferdinand Verbiest, his opportunity. In 1668, emperor Shunzhi's successor Kangxi, now fourteen years old, dispensed with his regents. In December of that year a copy of Yang's new calendar came into the hands of Verbiest, who noticed several mistakes and bravely sent a memorial to the young emperor, challenging Yang to prove certain points. Kangxi gave Verbiest from December 27 until February 1, 1669 to validate his criticism. Verbiest was able to do this to the satisfaction of Kangxi, who gave the priest his rival's post in the Board of Astronomy.

Emperor Kangxi was by all accounts an outstanding ruler, a man brought up as a Manchu — his Chinese was imperfect — yet sensitive to Chinese sophistication. A strong relationship grew between the emperor and the priest. According to Verbiest: "I used to go to the palace at break of day, and did not quit until three or four in the afternoon; and during this time I remained with the emperor reading and explaining . . . Very often he would keep me to dinner, and entertain me with most dainty dishes, served on a gold plate. To appreciate fully these marks of friendship shown me by the emperor, a European must remember that the sovereign is revered as a divinity and is scarcely ever seen by anyone, especially not by foreigners."[6]

For his part, Kangxi requested that Verbiest refit the imperial observatory, and the priest also introduced the thermometer and cast some 320 cannons. Verbiest did not feel comfortable about these cannons, so to absolve his conscience each cannon was named after a saint and sprinkled with holy water. Sometimes Verbiest was called on by Kangxi to help with a visiting embassy. At a high point of the friendship, Verbiest accompanied the imperial party on two trips to the northern hunting grounds; then at least twice Kangxi visited the fathers at home in the city. This great patronage led to the emperor signing the Decree of the Board of Rites in 1692, in which he granted protection to the missionaries. Sadly, Verbiest died in 1688 at the age of 65, before he could celebrate his achievement. At the emperor's bidding his funeral was attended by some of the grandest dignitaries of the court, and he was buried in the Jesuit Cemetery alongside Ricci.

Although the fathers were at last openly recognized by the emperor, jealousy and distrust of them was growing. Many believed they were spies intent on furthering the wishes of Europe to invade the Great Within. As for Kangxi, he showed favor to the Jesuits because of their many useful skills, but he had no interest in embracing their religion. It seemed that the way to lead the Chinese people to salvation was not, after all, to be found either through the stars or in the casting of cannons. When the Papacy started agonizing over whether Chinese Christians could continue to perform the traditional rituals associated with the worship of ancestors, Kangxi's reaction was unequivocal: "As for the doctrine of the Occident . . . it is

Used by Kangxi when he studied mathematics, this gilt bronze calculator can help with addition, subtraction, multiplication and division.

contrary to the orthodoxy [of the Chinese classics] and it is only because its apostles have a thorough knowledge of the mathematical sciences that the State uses them — beware lest perhaps you forget that."[7]

If Christianity had a chance to take root in Chinese soil, it was blighted by what became known as the Rites Controversy. In an exchange of letters with Rome, Kangxi explained that the traditional rituals were of a secular nature. However, Pope Clement XI would not compromise, and in 1715 decreed that pure forms of European Christianity be observed, and forbade any Chinese rites such as worship at family shrines. Under pain of death, the missionaries were to abide by this ruling from the Holy See. Kangxi's answer to this dictum was exquisitely patronizing. "All that can be said about this decree is that one asks oneself how the Europeans, ignorant and contemptible as they are, presume to deliver judgement on the lofty teachings of the Chinese, seeing that they [in

Emperor Kangxi at his studies.

Europe] know neither their manners, their customs, nor their letters . . . It is not advisable to allow the Europeans to proclaim their law in China. They must be forbidden to

speak of it; and in this way many difficulties and embarrassments will be avoided."[8] All Matteo Ricci's careful laying of foundations was undone. In 1717 decrees were issued which effectively banned the activities of Catholic missionaries, although Kangxi left enforcing them to his successor.

1 Louis J. Gallagher (trans.):
   China in the Sixteenth Century: The Journals of Matteo Ricci, 1583-1610
2 *China in the Sixteenth Century: The Journals of Matteo Ricci*
3 *China in the Sixteenth Century: The Journals of Matteo Ricci*
4 Memorial from the Board of Rites to the emperor, quoted in Maurice Collis: *The Great Within*
5 Quoted in Nigel Cameron: *Mandarins and Barbarians: Thirteen Centuries of Western Travelers in China*
6 *Mandarins and Barbarians: Thirteen Centuries of Western Travelers in China*
7 *Mandarins and Barbarians: Thirteen Centuries of Western Travelers in China*
8 Columba Cary-Elwes: *China and the Cross: Studies in Missionary History*

THE QING CONQUEST

In 1627, after a severe drought, a local uprising flared and spread to the provinces. As the rebellion rumbled on, a Manchurian tribe began to threaten China's northern frontier. These Manchu tribesmen had made three breaches in the Great Wall since the early 1620s but failed actually to cross it. The dire consequences of Yongle's transfer of the imperial capital to the northeast now became glaringly apparent. Beijing, only forty miles from several passes in the Great Wall, was dangerously exposed to enemy attack. As the Mongols had shown, the frontier city would be the first to fall to an invading nomad army, and the natural choice for the invaders' capital once their conquest of China was complete. Most significantly, Beijing was quite distant from the empire's real center of culture, commerce and wealth — the southern provinces around the Yangzi.

Adam Schall was ordered by his Ming masters in 1643 to recommend improve-

Hunting a hare. Originally mounted tribesmen, the Manchus placed emphasis on horsemanship, shooting and archery.

ments to the fortifications of Beijing. He was not sanguine about the effectiveness of the city's defenses, and he was to be proved right. By April 1644 Beijing found itself caught between the rebels and the Manchus. The rebels under the command of Li Zicheng arrived first, setting torch to the city and threatening the Palace. In a last-ditch attempt to save the throne, a Chinese general offered the Manchus an alliance against the rebels, and opened a gate to the eastern pass of the Great Wall, letting the Manchus in. As the rebels fled, the Manchus found themselves in possession of the undefended capital and decided to stay. Chongzhen, the last Ming emperor, deserted by his ministers, committed solitary suicide by hanging himself behind the Forbidden City. And so the Mandate of Heaven passed, almost by accident, to the new occupants of the capital city. The Manchu dynasty called itself Qing (Pure). Two brilliant emperors — the second and the fourth — consolidated Qing rule: Kangxi, who inherited the throne when he was only eight years old, and his grandson Qianlong, whose reign was one of the longest and most prosperous in Chinese history.

INNER COURT

As we walk from palace to palace down those long corridor streets imprisoned between

the high pink walls which are so characteristic of the Forbidden City, we seem to feel ghosts

follow us wherever we go. Phantoms move across the flagstones silently in satin shod feet.

Voices whisper in the shadows. Surely something remains of those invisible presences —

the endless procession of eunuchs, court ladies and serving maids, who,

in the days of the Empire, were always passing, passing to and fro?

Juliet Bredon: *Peking*

THE DAILY ROUND

When China became a Republic in 1912, the last emperor Puyi was allowed to live on in the rear portion of the Forbidden City, but the new president had a wall built to separate the Outer and Inner Courts. Thus, at one stroke, the new masters of China severed the ex-emperor from the great ceremonial halls that had served as the backdrop for displays of imperial power.

We had earlier paused in our tour of the Forbidden City at the Hall of Preserving Harmony. Behind this last of the Three Front Halls is an open space with gates to the east, west and north. It is through the northern gate — the Gate of Heavenly Purity or Qianqingmen — that one passes from the Outer to the Inner Court. Here the emperor and his wives lived their private lives. This was where Puyi continued to hold illusory court after his abdication, for the Inner Court contains its own throne halls — the Three Rear Palaces, as they are collectively named — which mirror, though on a smaller scale, the three great halls of state of the Outer Court.

A magnificent carved marble causeway leads from the gate to the first of these: the Palace of Heavenly Purity, the emperor's residence during the Ming dynasty. His empress occupied the Palace of Earthly Tranquility (Kunninggong) to the north. Later this was abandoned in favor of the smaller buildings on the west; the Palace of Earthly Tranquility then became the

(Pages 56-57) Dawn breaking over a northern gate of the Forbidden City. (Opposite) Inside the Hall of Mental Cultivation. (Above) Roofs of the Inner Court.

venue for imperial honeymoons, a section of it being used as the nuptial chamber for three days after the wedding. In the Qing dynasty, the central section of the palace was given over to secret religious ceremonies. When the Manchus conquered China in 1644 they brought their own shamanistic cult with them and, right up to the fall of the dynasty, sacrifices to the spirits and the associated mystic rites and dances continued to be conducted alongside their adopted Buddhist worship.

In between the two rear palaces is the Hall of Union (Jiaotaidian), a square, single-eaved building in which the twenty-five imperial seals have been preserved since 1746. It is rather simply furnished with a lacquered throne-chair and some panels of inscription. The dominating panel, hung on the back wall above the chair, has an inscription with only two characters, *Wu Wei* (or "inaction"), a Taoist precept for human conduct which advocates letting things take their own course, and governing by doing nothing that goes against nature. The hall also contains a bronze clepsydra and a huge chiming clock made in 1798.

A labyrinth of halls and courtyards lies east and west of these inner palaces, rectangular blocks of buildings surrounded by walls. The predilection for symmetry, apparent in the Outer Court, can be observed here as well, but the edifices are closer together, and there is enough irregularity in the plan for the visitor to feel that this part of the complex was purposely built to a human scale. A bird's eye view would reveal layers of yellow roofs fitting one into another, and separated only by long narrow alleys. In design the halls of the Inner Court, apart from the three rear palaces, are actually the traditional Chinese courtyard house writ large. And like those courtyard houses, they consist of a central open space flanked by halls on the sides and at the back, and sometimes a surprising, concealed garden screened off by walls. Each group of halls and courtyard comprised a separate apartment, a clearly defined living space for the emperor, his empress, consorts and concubines, so that they all had, as it were, their own house. All, that is, except the junior concubines: those below the fourth rank had to find a billet with one or another of the senior concubines. Every "household" had its own kitchen, with its complement of cooks and servants, and the most comfortable room would be a "warm chamber" where the *kang,* running along one wall, imparted enough heat for its occupants to withstand the cold of Beijing winters. (In the houses of northern China, the *kang* — a raised platform heated from below — was installed for the occupants to sleep on in winter. Short-legged tables, which can be seen in the furnished rooms of the Forbidden City today, were put on *kangs* for use during the day.)

Of course, in the five hundred years that the Palace was occupied, the same buildings were used for different purposes at different times. Yongle lived in the Palace of Heavenly Purity, but at the end of Kangxi's reign the Hall of Mental Cultivation (Yangxindian) came to be preferred. The empress dowager Cixi, who effectively ruled China from 1861 to 1908, lived successively in the Palace of Concentrated Beauty (Chuxiugong) and the Palace of Peaceful Longevity (Ningshougong, on the eastern side of the Inner Court), with stints in the summer palace of Yiheyuan (Garden for Cultivating Harmony). Cixi favored the Palace of Concentrated Beauty, many believe, because it was in one of its pavilions that she gave birth to her son and future emperor. But often one residence was changed for another because it had become inauspicious — perhaps a death had occurred there, or an accident. "There were several buildings," wrote Princess Der Ling, a Manchu noblewoman who was lady-in-waiting to the empress dowager in 1903, "which were not used at all; these were sealed and nobody seemed to know what they contained, or whether they contained anything at all. Even Her Majesty said she had never been inside these buildings, as they had been sealed for many years. Even the entrance to the enclosure containing these buildings was always closed, and this was the only occasion that any of us ever even passed through. They were quite different in appearance from any other buildings in the Palace, being very dirty and evidently of great age. We were commanded not to talk about the place at all."[1]

Closed doors were encountered everywhere in the Forbidden City, keeping intruders out and its inmates safe. Anyone caught inside without proper authorization incurred a hundred blows of the watchman's cudgel. Since at any one time scores of sentries patrolled the walls, and as many watchmen guarded the gates, it is surprising how often this punishment was dealt out. But then one only had to be caught loitering near the gates and the blows would rain down. If a trespasser dared to enter the imperial apartments, he would be put to death at once.

In a very real sense the Forbidden City was a fortress, and defense of it devolved on several garrisons of guards. At dusk security was boosted in a number of ways. Puyi remembered particularly the eerie call sent up by the eunuchs at lock-up time. A nervous child, he thought their high-pitched cry "Draw the bolts, mind the lanterns!", echoing across the Inner Court, a warning to the ghosts and demons that would appear round the windows and doors as soon as darkness fell. The eunuchs were followed by the

(Opposite) A garden in the Palace of Benevolent Tranquility.

officials in charge of the keys, making a final round to inspect the doors.

In fact, the Forbidden City shut down only for a few brief hours during the night. Messengers continued to come and go until the early hours of the morning. As an additional security measure, anyone entering or leaving the Palace at night was required to show one half of a specially issued tally; the other matching half was kept in locked boxes at the main gate-houses. A pair, with the two characters "Imperial Edict" engraved in relief and intaglio, had to be matched before the possessor would be allowed to pass through.

Visitors at night invariably included couriers. It was the custom during the Qing dynasty for memorials from the six boards to be delivered at midnight. As already mentioned, memorials were reports and petitions submitted to the emperor by officials. Generally they were of two kinds: memorials dealing with public matters, and those raising personal concerns. Both were carried by couriers and delivered to the Grand Secretariat. The grand secretaries then drafted their recommended courses of action on yellow slips of paper for the emperor's perusal and comment. All the documents were afterward copied

— in Chinese and Manchu scripts during the Qing dynasty — and filed.

By the time emperor Kangxi was on the throne, a third kind of memorial came to be favored. Imperial China was an autocracy, and keeping power centralized

A passage between doors in the Palace of Heavenly Purity.

required an effective intelligence network. Kangxi, like his Ming predecessors, made extensive use of the memorial system, but it was undeniable that confidentiality was

almost impossible when the documents passed through so many hands. The variant which Kangxi introduced, the so-called "palace memorials," reached the emperor in a sealed box. They were generally concerned with the weighty aspects of government, such as internal security, military policy and fiscal, ethnic and religious affairs, but even very private matters could also be communicated in this way: Kangxi is known to have received secret memorials from trusted officials about the dissolute behavior of his son and heir Yinreng. Appropriately the "top secret" and sensitive palace memorials were sometimes written on small folded sheets, small enough to be held and read in the palm of the hand. Often the emperor replied personally, writing interlinear comments on them in vermilion ink. They would then be sealed and returned to the original memorialists, who were required, after reading, to return the memorials to Beijing for the imperial files. Kangxi was punctilious about the confidentiality of palace memorials: he divulged neither the contents nor his remarks. "The palace memorials were read by me in person, and I wrote the rescripts on them myself, with my left hand if my right was paining me too much."[2] It was a remarkably fast and efficient method for the emperor to keep himself in touch with the most important government issues of the day.

Two hours after their arrival, the memorial couriers would be sent on their way, carrying a batch of rescripts copied out by the grand secretaries earlier that day, back to the offices of the six boards. Soon afterward the Inner Court would be astir, for the emperor rose at five. Eunuchs, the only other adult males to have remained inside the Palace after dark, scurried along the passages about their tasks. There would be no grand audiences or sacrifices, but it was still going to be a busy day.

"All propitiousness, Your Majesty" was the eunuchs' greeting to the emperor when he woke. They helped him wash, and served him tea with milk, and a fortifying broth made with birds' nest and crystallized sugar. A short period of prayer and contemplation followed. In all of the emperor's apartments, there would be a small Buddhist shrine to which he invariably repaired after rising, to light a few sticks of incense and recite a sutra. Then he might read from *Records of the Ancestors,* the official history of the dynasty; perhaps there

were lessons from the past to be gleaned.

Most people have a life in which their work is superimposed. The emperor had work in which life was a part. Regulations laid down through the ages governed every aspect of his existence. Take

(Top) Gilded copper tally, with "Imperial Edict" engraved on each half. (Bottom) Palace memorial from Suzhou, annotated by emperor Kangxi in vermilion ink.

his clothes, for example. Dressing by the rules was very much part of the decorum that marked him as a superior man and

responsible monarch. He had summer and winter wardrobes, and he changed from one to the other on a set day of the year. Which items of the imperial wardrobes he wore and when he wore them were all carefully cataloged, so that we know, for instance, that on the sixth day of the second lunar month in 1754 the Qianlong emperor put on a sable-trimmed satin hat and a traveling robe of blue silk with white fox fur. Over the robe he wore a short unlined garment of black leopard skin, and round his waist a yellow woven belt hung with a coral-decorated pouch. White cotton socks, heavy brocade leggings and sheepskin-lined satin boots completed his attire.

Traveling only as far as the Palace of Heavenly Purity for a routine audience, though, the emperor would have been dressed in his yellow court robe. He had by now eaten the first of his two main meals of the day. It had been served where he happened to be — in one of the small chambers off his bedroom — and it was as usual a surfeit of dishes, most of which were returned to the imperial kitchen untasted. He usually dined alone. If he wanted company, he might summon a concubine to join him.

She would not sit, of course, but stand by his table, all the while pressing delicacies upon him, and being able to serve him in this manner would have been regarded as a very high honor. We have Puyi to thank for this account of a meal in the Hall of Mental Cultivation, where he lived after abdicating: "There were special terms to refer to the emperor's eating and it was absolutely forbidden to fail to use them correctly. Food was called not 'food' but 'viands'; eating was called 'consuming viands'; serving the meal was 'transmitting the viands'; and the kitchen was the 'imperial viands room'. When it was time to eat (and the times of the meals were not set but were whenever the emperor felt like eating), I would give the command 'Transmit the viands' to the eunuchs standing in the main hall of the palace in which I lived and they would pass it on to the eunuchs standing on duty outside the hall; these would in turn call it out to the eunuchs of the 'imperial viands room' waiting in the Western Avenue of the Forbidden City. Thus my order went straight to the kitchens, and before its echoes had died away a procession rather of the sort that used to take a bride's trousseau to her groom's house had already issued from the 'viands room'. It

was made up of an imposing column of several dozen neatly dressed eunuchs hurrying to the Palace [or Hall] of Mental Cultivation with seven tables of various sizes and scores of red-lacquered boxes painted with golden dragons. When they reached the main hall they handed their burdens to young eunuchs wearing white sleeves who laid out the meal in an eastern room of the palace.

"Usually there were two tables of main dishes with another one of chafing-dishes added in winter; there were three tables of cakes, rice and porridge respectively; and there was another small table of salted vegetables. All the crockery was imperial yellow porcelain with dragon designs and the words 'Ten thousand long lives without limit' painted on it. In winter I ate from silver dishes placed on top of porcelain bowls of hot water. Every dish or bowl had a strip of silver on it as a precaution against poison, and for the same reason all the food was tasted by a eunuch before it was brought in. This was called 'appraising the viands'. When everything had been tasted and laid out and before I took my place a young eunuch would call out 'Remove the covers'. This was the signal for four or five other junior eunuchs to take the silver lids off all the food dishes, put them in a large box and carry them out. I then began to 'use the viands'."[3]

Four bearers carried the emperor in his sedan chair to the Palace of Heavenly Purity, and here the business of the day would begin. There were memorials to be read and rescripts to be written. The names of officials requesting an audience had already been presented at breakfast; now these officials would be summoned in hierarchical order. More often than not, officials from all the six boards would wait on His Majesty, first presenting a memorial and then, on their knees, making a verbal report as well. The emperor's decision on any matter brought to his attention would then be made known in an edict.

The audience over, there was more paperwork to be tackled. Particularly in times of war, memorials would come thick and fast for the emperor's urgent attention. Qianlong never failed to devote time to such communiqués: during the campaigns against the Dzungars and the suppression of the Jinchuan rebels, for example, he would spend the whole day dealing with memorials.

It was only at the afternoon meal, taken around two o'clock, that the emperor could turn his mind to rest and pleasure. A creature of flesh and blood, after all, he had his indulgences, but in general they were limited to the sort of cerebral pursuits deemed proper for a man of cultivation. We have already said that

emperors were expected to conform to the Confucian ideal: that meant displaying a fondness for enquiry and study, and a penchant for such scholarly preoccupations as calligraphy and painting. Kangxi, we know, was indefatigable in his pursuit of learning. Both he and Qianlong composed poetry and showed good taste in painting and calligraphy. They did, however, manage to vary the tedium of living in the Forbidden City by spending summers in their hunting parks and making elaborate tours of the empire.

Less conscientious rulers might have spent rather more time with their concubines. Still, though the emperor was undoubtedly a human being beneath his dragon robe, many court regulations constrained him where women were concerned. For one thing, he could never satisfy a passing fancy, since in selecting a bedmate for the night, he had to follow a procedure hallowed by custom. At his second meal of the day, his eunuchs would bring in a silver tray of nameplates in the form of bamboo slips with their tips painted in green. Each one bore the name of an imperial wife. The emperor's hand would hover, then turn over the *shanpai* of his choice. It is true that he generally had many women to choose from, but it

Lijingxuan, a pavilion in the Palace of Concentrated Beauty, where emperor Tongzhi was born.

does not take a great deal of imagination to see that such sexual pleasure as he might have enjoyed must have been limited, when the course of coupling was apparently so regimented. Indeed, with his empress it must often have been merely dutiful, since by the law of his ancestors the Qing emperor must bed his empress for a month after the wedding and for three nights every New Year.

Obviously all the seemingly petty rules contained in the family law were calculated to ensure the continuance of the dynastic line. If, despite the timely consummation, the empress failed to conceive, the consorts and concubines might be more productive. The law was firm on another point — on no account should his spouses divert the emperor from his responsibilities. His bedmate was therefore never permitted to stay till the morning. While he sank under his embroidered quilt, she would slip away to spend the rest of the night on her own in an antechamber. Would she, or the emperor, have been troubled by this? Probably not. They would simply have accepted that this way of doing things was the unquestioned law of their ancestors.

1   Princess Der Ling: *Two Years in the Forbidden City*
2   Jonathan D. Spence: *Emperor of China: Self-Portrait of K'ang-hsi*
3   Aisin-Gioro Pu Yi: *From Emperor to Citizen*

慧賢皇貴妃

THE GILDED CAGE

Written in collaboration with TANG YINIAN, *Researcher, First Historical Archives of China*

Once a year, on the ninth day of the ninth lunar month, the festival of Chongyang, it is a Chinese custom to ascend to higher ground for a picnic and to drink a cup of chrysanthemum wine. So it was with the women of the imperial court. To mark the festival, they would take a turn in the Imperial Garden at the northern end of the Forbidden City and climb the Hill of Accumulated Elegance (Duixiushan). Did they, peering over the walls, yearn for the freedom of their childhood and remember their families, whom they would never see again? Perhaps Jia Yuanchun, a character in the famous eighteenth-century Chinese novel of manners *Hong Lou Meng (A Dream of Red Mansions)*, spoke for them all when she said, "How much happier are those whose home is a hut in the field, who eat salt and pickles and wear clothes of cotton, than she who is endowed with wealth and rank but separated from her flesh and blood?"

When we try to conjure up a detailed picture of the life of imperial concubines, we find little help beyond a list of high-sounding names and titles — Esteemed, Filial, Virtuous, Wise. Their inner history is a blank. No fragment of journals or diaries, if they existed, has been preserved. It would in any case have been considered unseemly to commit private

thoughts to paper as, say, Sei Shōnagon did in her *Pillow Book*. Nevertheless, between the lines of official records, and in the pages of a novel such as *Hong Lou Meng,* some hint of their plight does come through to us. We

(Opposite) Huixian, Imperial Consort to emperor Qianlong, in court dress. (Above) An imperial concubine's outer robe, in satin with embroidered butterflies and magnolias.

can put ourselves in the shoes of a girl on the brink of womanhood, entering the Forbidden City for the first time.

This girl is a Manchu, the daughter of a

high-ranking Bannerman, so the summons from the Palace is not unexpected. She has always known that every three years the Manchu Bannermen's unmarried daughters between the ages of thirteen and seventeen must submit themselves for selection as imperial concubines. The Manchus were descendants of the Jurchen tribes who lived beyond the northeast fringes of the Chinese empire. In 1601, when the Ming emperor Wanli still sat on the throne, a chieftain of the Manchus organized his tribesmen into four companies of three hundred men each, and identified them by banners of different colors, colors which were also later replicated on their formal suits of armor. (The Qing traditionally dated their dynasty from the time of this founding chieftain, Nurhaci.) Functioning as administrative as much as military units, the Banners became the basis of the Manchus' strength, not only in their takeover of China but also in their subjugation of the conquered territory. Expanded subsequently to eight units, the system in time included collaborators among the Mongolians and indigenous Han Chinese, and they too were enrolled under their own eight banners.

The system of selecting Bannermen's daughters for the Palace ensured the purity of the Manchu bloodline. Even though the Manchus were more or less physically indistinguishable from the northern Chinese, mixed marriages were banned. It is true that the rule was broken several times in practice — consider Kangxi, whose mother was the daughter of a Chinese Bannerman, and whose grandmother was a Mongolian. Still, every effort was made to uphold the rule. When a concubine candidate was inspected and interviewed by the emperor's mother or stepmother, it was her pedigree that was first examined. Then her horoscope was checked. Perhaps then they would consider her looks. But at this stage it was not a question of whether she would catch the emperor's eye. In fact, she might end her days a virgin, unless she was given in marriage to one of the imperial sons. And her widowhood, if she survived the emperor, would be spent in melancholy seclusion in the Palace of Benevolent Tranquility (Cininggong) or some other peripheral residence of the Forbidden City.

The recently introduced concubine would discover soon enough that, like many other institutions in the Forbidden City, a rigid hierarchy dictated the positions of imperial wives. Polygamy ensured many children, but a harem was inevitably a stultifying, unnatural and unhappy place. If anything, it resembled a prison, a cage with golden bars. In the brooding atmosphere of a house of lonely, jealous women, gossip and intrigue were the nearest there was to a breath of fresh air. It had long been recognized that, to prevent squabbling among the women, it was best to impose a pecking order so they knew where they stood. Hadn't the ancient classic *The Rites of Zhou* pronounced as much, when it prescribed for the Son of Heaven 120 wives, headed by the empress and divided into four other ranks?

By the Qing dynasty, the hierarchy consisted of the empress, one imperial consort, two high consorts, four consorts, six imperial concubines, eight *guiren* and two further ranks of lesser concubines, which could be as many as the emperor wished. Their names can be found in the huge yellow volumes of the Genealogical Record of the Imperial Clan, or the Jade Document, as it is commonly called. The Jade Document listed 189 imperial spouses between the eleven Qing rulers excluding Puyi, the last emperor. But these were only the officially recognized wives. Kangxi had thirty-eight wives according to the document, but from other sources it is evident that he had as many as fifty-five. The unrecorded seventeen were presumably of low birth, and not considered respectable enough to be granted official status. More to the point, they had produced no children. Emperor Guangxu, on the other hand, had only one empress and two concubines, although he did die relatively young, and might be supposed to have had no time to marry more.

It would be no exaggeration to say that the newly selected imperial concubine could look forward only to a pallid and emotionless existence. Yet with what mingled fear and excitement she had awaited her first encounter with the emperor! His favor had been made known at lunch, when the *shanpai* with her name had been placed face down on the shiny silver tray. A eunuch had padded softly into her room to inform her. That evening she could hardly bear to listen to the whispered chatterings of her maids when they brought the hot water for her bath, so nervous was she at the prospect that lay ahead. It was a powdered and scented, if tremulous, beauty who was led, like a lamb to the slaughter, toward the imperial bedchamber in the Hall of Mental Cultivation.

She had lain in the emperor's bed, and with luck she might bear him a child. The eunuchs waiting outside the bedchamber had recorded the visit; had seen to it that she did not stay long, so surely the emperor would rise refreshed to tackle the heavy business of state the next day. She had known, of course, that the emperor's private life, as much as his public one, was governed by rules enshrined in ancestral family law. Decorum and restraint in his personal conduct was essential to the order and well-being of the empire. All the same, it had been unsatisfactory, even rather disillusioning, to have sealed her fate in those brief embraces. Shortly afterward, the eunuchs had escorted her to a room on the

other side of the imperial bedchamber. Since the palace doors were locked, she had to spend the rest of the night there.

Where sexual convention was concerned, the Qing court could never quite forget the weakness of the emperor Shunzhi, whose love of a woman had imperiled the empire. Archival records show that, one day in the tenth lunar month of 1660, the court held Buddhist rites on both land and water for the soul of a deceased concubine. Dong'e, originally Shunzhi's sister-in-law and just twenty-two years old when she died, had been the emperor's favorite. The Jesuit astronomer at the Qing court, Adam Schall, noted in his memoirs that after Dong'e died, the emperor, wracked by passionate grief, evinced no interest in anything and repeatedly attempted suicide. The courtiers had to watch over him day and night to stop him taking his own life. So that she would not lack attendants to serve her in the nether world, thirty eunuchs and palace maids killed themselves for her. Elsewhere in his memoirs, Schall spoke of emperor Shunzhi falling in love with the wife of a Manchurian soldier, whose convenient death, either from jealousy or suicide, left the widow free to enter the

(Left) Noble ladies wearing flowers in their hair, by Jin Tingbiao. (Pages 72-73) Four from a series of twelve portraits of beauties, thought to be concubines of the future emperor Yongzheng.

Palace as a high-ranking concubine.

When Shunzhi died, his empress and senior ministers saw to it that no opportunity would ever be given for future emperors to fall prey to such violent infatuation again. Their precaution resulted in a number of regulations governing the selection of imperial wives, the positions of concubines and indeed the marriage bed — a somewhat heavy-handed response to what had been no more than a love affair, but it sprang from what were perceived as the overriding demands of protecting the dynasty. For some two hundred years afterward, emperors and their wives allowed protocol to rule their emotional life, all apparently for the good of the state.

Again and again we find echoes of this dread of women, of their ability to enthrall and usurp power in times of imperial weakness. Perhaps in an attempt to divide and rule, emperor Qianlong revised the palace protocol and defined the imperial wives' roles as follows: the empress was "to direct internal affairs from the central palace," with the consorts and concubines giving support from the two wings of the Inner Court, the eastern and western palaces. In fact, this was a meaningless injunction. The empress did indeed enjoy high status: when her title was officially conferred she was given a golden

(Opposite) A painted walkway in one of the eastern palaces in the Inner Court.

book and a golden seal, and at New Year she held court for all those who were required to pay their respects to her. But she did not manage "internal affairs" as a housewife might run her home — that was the duty of the chief eunuch.

The lessons from the past were heeded too. The court was ever conscious that, given the opportunity, factions could form around a favorite concubine. To prevent any attempt to annex power from the throne, concubines were isolated from their kinsmen. After entering the Palace, contact with their parents and siblings was more or less severed. Their families could not visit, nor were the concubines permitted to return to their parental homes without special permission from the emperor.

There is an evocative description of just such a reunion in *Hong Lou Meng*. A daughter of the Jia family, Yuanchun, is the fortunate imperial concubine. When, by the magnanimity of a gracious emperor, her family's application for her to visit is approved, the house makes lavish preparations to receive her. A new garden is built, complete with halls and pavilions. In one of them,

". . . painted phoenix and coiling dragon
flapped and fluttered on drapes and
curtains,
gold and silver-work gleamed and glinted,
jewels and gems made a fiery sparkle,
subtle incenses smouldered in brazen

censers,
'everlastings' blossomed in china vases . ."[1]

Her arrival is heralded by pairs of eunuchs leading a procession, a colorful calvacade of more eunuchs — some carrying embroidered banners, others ceremonial pheasant-feather fans, with yet another holding a huge golden parasol, "hanging from its curve-topped shaft like a great drooping bell-flower" trailing close behind. The imperial visitor's traveling wardrobe in boxes comes next, followed by eunuchs carrying "her rosary, her embroidered handkerchief, her spittoon, her fly-whisk, and various other items." Finally, her gold-topped palanquin with phoenixes embroidered on its yellow curtains, borne by eight eunuchs, comes in sight. All her family, including Grandmother Jia, drop onto their knees in welcome.

The ceremonial greetings and exchanges over, Yuanchun is at last reunited with her grandmother, a meeting attended by both smiles and tears. The imperial concubine eventually summons up enough composure to say, "It hasn't been easy, winning this chance of coming back among you after all those years since I was first walled up in That Place. Now that we are seeing each other at last, we ought to talk and be cheerful, not waste all the time crying! I shall be leaving again in no time at all, and Heaven only knows when I shall have another chance of seeing you!"

Yuanchun's meeting with her father is, however, much more formal. He has to stand outside her room, with a door-curtain between them. "Now that she was the emperor's woman, this was the nearest to her he could ever hope to get." It is at this moment that the bitter lament quoted in the first paragraph of this chapter is wrung from her.

Yuanchun dies at forty-three, without issue. In accordance with precedent, she is awarded a posthumous title, Illustrious and Chaste Imperial Concubine. Having children, in any case, could be a mixed blessing for imperial wives. It is true that they were elevated in rank immediately after giving birth, yet maternal fulfillment was often denied them. The baby princes and princesses were usually taken away from their mothers to be raised by wet-nurses and eunuchs. Because as an infant he contracted smallpox, the dreaded disease that had carried off his father, Kangxi was sent away from the Palace and looked after by a nurse. In less unusual circumstances, the children were brought to wait upon their mothers once in the morning and once in the evening — a ritual not calculated to further bonding and inspire deep affection.

Without the duties of motherhood and the constant society of husband and family, what did the women of the Palace do? How did they idle away the time? They did what all women of leisure do — they took enor-mous pains over their appearance, gossiped and bickered with each other and indulged in harmless little pleasures (painting perhaps, or playing dominoes, or listening to opera or keeping birds). Their days passed with the strange and deadly slowness of acute mo-notony. A eunuch who served the dowager consort Jingyi (Esteemed and Virtuous), the widow of emperor Tongzhi (reigned 1862-74), recalled: "I was one of two hundred and sixty eunuchs in her Palace of Eternal Spring (Changchungong). We were more numer-ous than the maidservants. Between us we had the care of our mistress and her kitchen, larder, dispensary, shrine and all the other rooms she used.

"The maidservants were busy in the morning, bustling about in the bedchamber, helping to wash, bath and dress the dowager consort, making the bed and emptying the chamberpot.

"At eight o'clock the dowager consort would breakfast, and afterward, for half an hour or so, say a rosary. Then she would have some tea and perhaps smoke her waterpipe. A light lunch would be served at one, and a short nap taken in the early afternoon. She would get up at three and have her dinner at four. Dinner over, she usually said another rosary. If the weather was fine, she would take a stroll in the garden attended by eunuchs and maids. Or she might play a board game. Sometimes, to amuse her, a eunuch told a story or the latest jokes. One or two of the young eunuchs were particularly good mimics, and could entertain us all by barking like a dog or mewing like a cat. At other times, a piece of news from the outside world would be relayed by a eunuch who'd been on an errand outside the Palace gates. The evenings would pass in this torpid way until around ten o'clock, when she would have a late snack and retire to bed.

"Two maidservants and six eunuchs kept watch by her chamber every night. I've heard it said that the average cost of living for each imperial concubine amounted to two hundred taels of silver a day. But what an insipid and pointless existence it was!

"Then there's Xuantong's [Puyi's] em-press. Her everyday life was just as dull, though she did have her books and painting. Later she took to smoking opium. Every meal was rounded off by eight pipes of the drug, served to her by a eunuch on his knees. This way, she exchanged the numbing tedium of her life for another kind of ob-livion."[2]

1 The quotations from *Hong Lou Meng,* except for the first, are from Cao Xueqin: *The Story of the Stone,* translated by David Hawkes

2 *Wan Qing gongting shenghuo jianwen*

PIGEON WHISTLES

WANG SHIXIANG

There is a poignant image, captured in a portrait, of an imperial concubine looking out of the window of her pavilion at a pair of twittering birds. It is not known if the artist intended these to be wild birds settling momentarily in a palace garden, or pet ones released from their cages for their daily exercise. But a familiar sight in old Beijing was of birds being tossed up in the air by their owners to fly up into the sunlight. Keeping birds as pets has a long tradition in China. Raising pigeons to hear them make music is an even more enchanting pursuit, and one particularly identified with the capital city.

The ladies of the court, looking up above the scarlet walls of their golden prison, would have seen pigeons wheeling overhead, but those birds filled the sky not only with their fluttering wings, but also with song. The music in the heavens swelled and shrank, became distant and then near, suddenly accelerating and as abruptly slowing. And the women would have known that such delightful sounds could only have been produced by currents of air caught up by whistles tied to the pigeons' tails. Their brothers and uncles might well have been pigeon-fanciers, for many of the Manchu Bannermen of Beijing, a privileged class with wealth and leisure at its disposal, became connoisseurs of various esoteric sports and amusements.

A Record of Annual Events in Yanjing, published in 1906, recommended: "When it is time to fly pigeons one must attach bamboo whistles above their tails, or gourds can also be made into whistles. Gourds may be of various sizes; and whistles can be of three or five pipes in a row, with a different number of openings. They give out notes of various pitches to the delight of ear and mind."

The pigeons, thus equipped, can be released to fly long distances, in which case they vanish in almost no time, and only the ringing music of the whistles, much later in the day, will warn the owner of their return. More frequently, the flock is trained to circle around their base, spiraling higher and higher up to the clouds and then wheeling lower and lower over the owner's house. In this exercise the sounds become unusually melodious when the birds bank left and right. Best of all, there is the moment when the whistles are suddenly silenced as the birds unexpectedly drop down out of the air, then resume as they gain height again. It is one of the strangest and loveliest pleasures to be encountered around Beijing.

(Above) One of the twelve portraits of beauties.

EUNUCHS AND MAIDSERVANTS

Written in collaboration with TANG YINIAN, *Researcher, First Historical Archives of China*

"At home I sit in a daze and lost, abroad I know not where I am going. Whenever I think of this shame the sweat drenches the clothes on my back. I am fit only to be a slave guarding the women's apartments: better that I should hide away in the farthest depths of the mountains. Instead I go on as best I can, putting up with whatever treatment is meted out to me, and so complete my degradation."[1]

This was China's first great historian, Sima Qian, writing in the second century BC about his emasculation, a punishment for offending the emperor. Bitterly conscious of his shame, he sublimated his anguish in an intellectual endeavor that resulted in the work *Historical Records,* a masterpiece and a model for all the Chinese historians who followed him.

Eunuchs in the Qing court had no such recourse. Unlike Sima Qian and other eunuchs whose mutilation was a form of punishment — either for a crime or because they were prisoners of war — most of the eunuchs in the Forbidden City had actually volunteered for castration. Such a drastic choice of career was generally dictated by harsh economic necessity. Here is an old eunuch, castrated by his own choice, speaking: " . . . It seemed a little thing to give up

one pleasure for so many. My parents were poor, yet by suffering that small change I could be sure of an easy life in surroundings

*(Opposite) Enclosed courtyard in the Inner Court.
(Above) Statuette of an old eunuch.*

of beauty and magnificence; I could aspire to intimate companionship with lovely women unmarred by their fear or distrust of me. I could even hope for power and wealth of my own. With good fortune and diligence, I

might grow more rich and powerful than some of the greatest officials in the empire."[2]

Regular recruitment of around a hundred eunuchs a year was organized by the Neiwufu or Imperial Household Department, which also arranged the employment of maidservants. Similar to the system under which imperial concubines were selected, there was an institution for bringing teenage girls to work in the Palace as maids. But in contrast to imperial concubines, these girls were from humbler backgrounds, being chosen from the families of bondservants, a hereditary cadre of imperial retainers. Bondservants, originally Chinese captives of war pressed into service by Nurhaci's conquering forces, were attached to the Banners and later served the Qing house loyally both in official posts in the provinces and as administrators in the Imperial Household Department.

The Imperial Household Department was a Manchu institution, but agencies that managed the complex domestic and financial aspects of the court had existed long before. The Forbidden City and its surrounding Imperial City exhibited all the ramifications of a real city, supporting a considerable population and satisfying most of their material needs from its own plants and workshops. There were spinners and weavers, carpenters and craftsmen, bakers and distillers, cleaners and carriers of fuel and food, not to mention the thousands of retainers responsible for the imperial stables, armory, dispensary and printing works, and the upkeep of the palace buildings and grounds. And what those plants and workshops could not supply themselves, the Palace collected under a tribute system that stretched to the outer reaches of the empire and beyond. From the Yangzi valley came the most succulent rice and from the mountains of Sichuan the hardiest timber. Lustrous pearls, delicate porcelain, the finest silks and the softest cotton flowed in from the south; sables, ermine and mink from the remote forests of the north; ginseng from Korea; and countless other prized offerings from the vassal states surrounding the Chinese empire.

The tribute and supplies converging on the Imperial City passed through the Imperial Household Department or, in the Ming dynasty, agencies organized into twenty-four offices and run largely by eunuchs. Emperor Wanli had upward of twenty thousand eunuchs on his staff. Some of them indeed "guarded the women's apartments," as was right and proper — in a closed community where polygamy was practiced, using eunuchs as servants ensured that the chastity of the harem women would never be called into question — but the majority were bureaucrats on equal footing with officials.

Opportunities for peculation and bribery were manifold. Moreover, in the Palace itself it was all too easy for eunuchs to insinuate themselves with their imperial master, to exploit their intimacy with him and to extend their influence beyond the domestic sphere. In the late Ming dynasty, the power of eunuchs at court, advanced also by the inertia of the emperors they served, reached such heights that the conduct of government was seriously undermined. Not surprisingly, they were subsequently blamed for the Ming dynasty's ruin.

The Qing rulers were not totally immune; the Shunzhi emperor fell under the influence of one called Wu Liangfu, though in a somewhat paradoxical move he denounced eunuchs in very strong terms. His edict, later engraved on an iron tablet which was installed in front of the Hall of Union, warned: "The inner palace system [of eunuchs] . . . could lead to disaster and turmoil if inappropriate appointments are made . . . If hereafter there is illegal interference in state affairs, usurping of power, accepting bribes . . . those involved will be put to death by dismemberment at once, without mercy."[3]

Examples of violation of Shunzhi's law were rare, for strict discipline was maintained, and keeping most of the eunuchs illiterate helped. Infractions were generally minor ones, such as gambling, stealing, fighting among themselves, smoking opium and attempting to escape. The usual punishments

Interior of the Palace of Concentrated Beauty, which empress dowager Cixi had refurbished for her fiftieth birthday.

were flogging with a bamboo cane, wearing the cangue (a wooden collar), a spell of hard labor or exile to the border regions. Rewards included a good salary by the standards of the time, end-of-year and festival day bonuses,

health care, retirement support and their own cemetery. If they pleased their masters, eunuchs might even be granted rather large amounts of gold and silver, an expensive fur robe or a house for their old age.

Favoritism was perhaps inevitable. Lonely and forgotten imperial wives, especially, might find a smooth-cheeked eunuch with winning ways both sympathetic and

attractive. Most stories of scandalous goings-on between mistress and eunuch centered on empress dowager Cixi. Gossip about her was rife in the early republican period; one rumor concerned the lady's *tendre* for a eunuch called Anzi. His arrival in the Palace, coinciding with the death of emperor Xianfeng (reigned 1851-61), found the twenty-eight-year-old widow particularly vulnerable, so that she

became thoroughly besotted with him. Courtiers began to wonder whether she made him serve her something more stimulating than tea. When it was time for her son Tongzhi to marry, Cixi entrusted Anzi with the commission of acquiring the wedding garments. But the poor eunuch was attacked and killed by a passing patrol on his way to the southern silk cities. Was he really a eunuch though? Ripping off his trousers, the attackers fell back in surprise at the sight of the "long spout on his teapot"!

Such stories were bound to circulate, but it was highly unlikely that anyone not a eunuch could have passed himself off as one. Not only were they inspected on recruitment, they were also required to submit themselves to a yearly physical check-up: there seems to have been a belief that the amputated organs would grow again.

Whatever the real story behind Anzi, favorite eunuchs there undoubtedly were, one of the most notable being Li Lianying, whom Cixi made an official of the second grade, an unprecedented honor for a eunuch. Still, no status, power or wealth could have quite compensated for the humiliation eunuchs felt as less than whole men. When, at the tender age of eight or nine, they were taken along to the house of Bi in the Hutong of Bookkeepers, or "Pocket-knife" Liu in Brick Hutong, they could not have known about society's revulsion for eunuchs, or of the money that would change hands or of a life from which there would be no escape. The Bi and Liu families were brokers appointed by the Imperial Household Department to recruit, screen and finally operate on prospective eunuchs. The posts were hereditary, and their skill, passed down from generation to generation, ensured a high rate of success. To be sure, the boys' families were always made to sign a contract just in case — a "Life or Death Document," they called it — but mortality was not so frequent as to stop the flow of volunteers.

After the wound had healed, the boys were interviewed by the chief palace eunuch and then assigned their duties. They were also assigned to a senior eunuch for training, for there were so many rules in the Palace that without practical instruction the novice could never hope to master them all. Take, for example, the titles: an emperor was addressed as "Lord of Myriad Years," an empress dowager as "Buddha." There were rules on kowtows, deportment, when to speak and when to hold their peace. Eunuchs-of-the-presence (those who attended the emperor) and members of the Service Office — the administrative and disciplinary branch — had to be accorded respect as well, for they had the highest status among the eunuchs. Some of the Service Office eunuchs were such adepts at trotting out the Qing ancestral family law that even the emperor had to be guided by them in matters of protocol. Eunuchs-of-the-presence were, of course, closest to the emperor. Apart from serving him his daily meals, guarding him and looking after his personal effects, they were the only people who could take a knife to the emperor, for they shaved the imperial forehead every ten days to enable him to wear his hair in the Manchu fashion. (The shaved forehead and pigtail was a hairstyle traditional to the Manchus; it was imposed on the indigenous Han Chinese and hated by many as a badge of subjugation.)

Qing regulations permitted a maximum of 3,300 eunuchs in the court at any one time; in fact, the corps always fell below that number, and in 1919 only about a thousand still remained to serve Puyi's reduced court at the rear of the Forbidden City. All but some fifty of them were expelled from the Palace on Puyi's orders in 1923. Many of the redundant eunuchs would have found refuge in temples to which they had donated money in better times. Some, no doubt, had saved enough to spend their retirement in comfort; the last of them died in Beijing aged 93 in 1996. For most of them time must have eventually blurred the memory of their sacrifice; even so, few, being Chinese, could have ever reconciled themselves to the ultimate deprivation. Our old eunuch, again, put this into words for us: "We have no wives, no sons to bear us grandsons and sacrifice at our tombs."[4]

1   Quoted in Cyril Birch (ed.): *Anthology of Chinese Literature*
2   John Blofeld: *City of Lingering Splendour*
3   This iron tablet is in the collection of the Palace Museum, Beijing.
4   *City of Lingering Splendour*

Note: *Hutong* is a term used in Beijing to refer to residential lanes or alleys.

A PALACE MAID REMEMBERS

She was a quiet, mousy sort of creature who never spoke above a murmur. When I first met her, she was already gray-haired, living alone in straitened circumstances in a *hutong* near Prospect Hill. Though we were neighbors, she was somewhat aloof and clearly reluctant to volunteer information about herself.

It was 1941. As summer turned to autumn, I began to know her a little better. I learned that she was from a Banner family, and had been a maid in the Palace. At eighteen she was given in marriage to a eunuch named Liu, but applied to return to the Palace within a year of the wedding. Cases like hers were extremely rare, and if she hadn't been exceptionally well liked by the empress dowager Cixi, she would never have been permitted to serve again. The second time round she remained another eight years. Her special charge was serving Cixi the waterpipe.

Those cool autumn evenings, sitting in her courtyard over a cup of tea, she would reminisce about her life in the Palace. Without being aware of it, she revealed exactly those contradictory feelings to which servants who both loved and hated their masters were prone. "We Banner people had always been privileged to serve the Palace. Girls who reached the age of thirteen or fourteen were picked from a register and summoned by the Neiwufu. Of course, not all girls were required to do this: those from grander families, or some who had friends in the Neiwufu, could arrange for their daughters to be exempt. But there were also those parents who wanted to give their daughters a chance to widen their horizons, to earn a couple of taels of silver each month and, regular as clockwork, to receive the bonuses granted by our mistresses on festival days and anniversaries. Also, the girls were likely to learn some manners and acquire a little polish. After all, a spell in the Palace raised your status, improving your chances of making a good marriage."

She sipped her tea and continued: "I was thirteen that summer when I was chosen for the Palace. We were allowed a few days to get used to our new life. Every morning I would be escorted to the Palace by my family, and at midday they would come and bring me home. And then one day, by arrangement, when I was alone in the house, a sedan chair was sent to take me into the Forbidden City. About thirty of us started on the same day. We were deposited at the Gate of Spiritual Valor (Shenwumen), where an old eunuch met us. Inside the Palace of Concentrated Beauty, we duly kowtowed in the direction of the empress dowager's bedchamber. From that moment on, we were considered part of the staff.

"Our first duty, after making the kowtow in the Palace of Concentrated Beauty, was to be presented to 'auntie.' Maids of an

---

A room in the Palace of Eternal Spring, one of the six western palaces, where empress dowager Cixi lived after Tongzhi came of age and officially assumed full powers of the throne.

earlier generation were known as aunties, and each new recruit was attached to a particular auntie for training. You see, palace maids usually served for four, five years. At seventeen or eighteen, we would be released so that we could marry. Aunties were approaching the end of their service and were usually anxious to bring on their replacements so that they could finally go home. Chances were they would train us properly, but that often meant endless scolding, beating and punishing. It got so that we would rather be beaten — the pain was soon over, after all. That was preferable to being made to kneel in a corner. You never knew how long you would remain there, on your knees. If anything, auntie was even harder to please than the empress dowager. Where I was concerned she was nearly as powerful: apart from punishing me, she could relegate me to the pool of general factotums undertaking all the most menial jobs in the Palace if she decided I had no potential.

"Mind you, though we were often beaten, we were never slapped on the face. There was an unwritten rule against this, I guess because a woman's face was her fortune. Eunuchs would be slapped, but never palace maids."

On other evenings, as shadows lengthened with the setting sun, she would sink into her memories again. When it was not quite dark enough to light the lanterns and start the evening meal, she would refill her teacup and settle down again to talk. "Our lives were governed by numerous regulations. I had to sleep on my side, not immodestly on my back. It took much beating before I learned to do so, I can tell you! Then we had to be so careful not to offend

Maids in the court of the deposed emperor Puyi.

the empress dowager's acute sense of smell. For years fish never passed my lips, and of course we shunned onion and garlic. We had to be completely unobtrusive. Our clothes were provided by the Palace. Come the spring, we would be measured for four sets of vest, blouse, robe and waistcoat. Except in October (the month of the empress dowager's birthday), when we were allowed to wear red, most of the year we were confined to a few colors — in spring and summer we dressed in pale blue or green, in autumn and winter a purplish brown. We wore our hair in a thick plait, tied at the end by a short red ribbon.

"We were taught to walk silently, with heads bowed and eyes lowered, to smile without showing teeth, to laugh without sound. Our features had to be composed so as not to give offense, which meant never showing our anger, frustration or sadness to the world. In the first couple of years, I was still young, I shed lots of tears. But one soon realized those were wasted tears. There was no one to see, no one to commiserate. What was the use of those tears?

"None of us learned to read, of course. What we were taught, though, was needlework. And those of us who showed particular aptitude could become pretty fair embroiderers. Then it would be a skill to set us up for life.

"Palace maids were really slaves. From morning till night we were at others' beck and call. Our status depended on that of our mistress — naturally the ones who served the empress or high consorts were a little above those who attended secondary concubines. When our mistresses were happy, we rejoiced with them. When they were depressed, we bore the brunt of their gloom. We servants clung to each other for emotional support. There was the

practice among maids and eunuchs of becoming each others' sworn sisters or brothers. Traditionally, eunuchs were recruited from the Han, while maids were drawn from the Banner people. Those poor thirteen- or fourteen-year-old eunuchs, made to do the most backbreaking jobs — Heaven knows how many times they banged their foreheads on the ground, what hardships they bore! They asked for nothing at all, only a bit of human kindness, to be able to call someone 'elder sister,' to capture in uttering those words a fleeting sense of family warmth."

In the darkness her voice was barely audible. "Our greatest joy was seeing our own family. I said, didn't I, that we all had our aunties? Within a few months of our entering the Palace, our aunties would help us find a 'godfather' among the older, more kindly or influential eunuchs. If we showed our respect for them as for our own fathers, they could make all the difference to our everyday life, perhaps by carrying messages to our families or doing the odd errand in the market. Many of the eunuchs lived near the north gate of the Forbidden City, in a *hutong* running along Beihai. They had contacts in the town and could arrange to bring our families to the Gate of Spiritual Valor to see us.

"The second of every month was family reunion day. A gate to the Forbidden City would be opened. Inside was a railing, and this was where we could stand to meet our dear ones, and where gifts could be handed over. Not all the maids enjoyed such a privilege. Some of them would not see their families for two or three years running. I was fortunate."

Extracted from Shen Yiling and Jin Yi: *Gongnu tan wang lu*

THE NEXT GENERATION

High up above the throne in the Palace of Heavenly Purity hangs a plaque; the four characters inscribed on it — *Zheng Da Guang Ming* — exhorts the emperor to be honorable and open. Though unremarkable in itself, as plaques and hangings can be seen in most of the halls of the Forbidden City, this plaque did for a time serve a special purpose. It concealed a secret testament.

To trace the events that led to the need for such a document, we may have to go back to 1654, the year of Kangxi's birth. It was not altogether a felicitous year for his mother, Consort Tong. She must have rejoiced at bearing a son, but the time of her confinement coincided with her fall from grace, her replacement in the emperor's affections by a rival. A month before the birth, emperor Shunzhi had become violently infatuated with his brother's wife, and Kangxi was barely one year old when the sixteen-year-old Dong'e discarded her husband and made her appearance at court. Dong'e then achieved rapid promotion to imperial consort, two grades above Consort Tong. The future Kangxi emperor was, of course, too young to know, but it must have been humiliating for his mother. Shortly after, more bad fortune befell Consort Tong: her infant son became ill.

The news the baby's wet-nurse brought one evening to the Palace of Admirable Benevolence (Jingrengong) sent a chill through Consort Tong — Kangxi was stricken with the smallpox, a disease feared

(Opposite) The throne room in the Palace of Heavenly Purity, with its "Honorable and Open" plaque. (Above) Emperor Kangxi in old age.

like the plague. By imperial law, all those afflicted with smallpox were banned from coming within forty miles of the city walls. There was nothing for it but to hustle the child out of the Forbidden City at least. Thus it was that, instead of growing up in the luxurious but stultifying atmosphere of

his mother's residence, Kangxi lived in the modest house of his wet-nurse Sun, on the bank of the Palace moat by the West Prosperity Gate (Xihuamen).

Later, his recovery from smallpox was strongly in his favor when the question of succession to the throne suddenly loomed. Kangxi was seven when Shunzhi himself contracted smallpox. By then the son borne by Dong'e, the emperor's favorite, had tragically died in his infancy. Shunzhi's eldest son had also died, while the youngest was still in swaddling clothes. The contest appeared to be between Kangxi and his stepbrother Fuquan. It did not take long for the courtiers to persuade Shunzhi that Kangxi was the wiser choice, not least because his immunity to smallpox considerably prolonged his life expectancy.

His own experience was probably in the forefront of Kangxi's mind when he named his two-year-old second son Yinreng as heir to the throne. When Yinreng was appointed, Kangxi was only twenty-two. There was no urgency in making such a decision, but Kangxi wished to prevent an unseemly scramble for the throne in the event of his own premature death, and he wanted no one to succeed him who had not been properly trained to the role. Yinreng's mother had

Target practice: to preserve Manchu traditions, Kangxi encouraged his sons to master archery and riding.

died in childbirth; instead of entrusting the task of rearing to others, Kangxi had the boy raised under his own eye. All the circumstances conspired to advance Yinreng in Kangxi's affections, and indeed on this son the emperor lavished all his expectations and love. " . . . Yin-jeng [Yinreng], Second Son, and my only son born to an empress, I named as Heir-Apparent at two, and raised myself in the Eastern Palace. When he was four and survived the smallpox, I sacrificed to Heaven and rewarded his doctors; I, the emperor, was his warm old nurse. I taught him to read myself, and entrusted his education to Chang Ying and Hsiung Tz'u-li, and had the wisest Hanlin scholars instruct him in morality . . . I instructed him in the principles of government . . . "[1]

Kangxi was to be severely disappointed. Yinreng grew up over-conscious of his unique position; he became spoilt, arrogant, licentious and cruel and, grossly indulged and flattered by his great-uncle Songgotu, he attempted a usurpation. Kangxi, though bitterly grieved at Yinreng's betrayal, forgave his son, and it was Songgotu whom he had executed — an action which brought the succession problem to a head.

In the following years Kangxi's suspicions about his son grew. And when they spent any time together, as on the long journeys Kangxi and his sons made to the Manchu homeland in the north, or down to the rich and cultured valley of the Yangzi River, the signs of Yinreng's brutality and recklessness were too evident to be ignored. Kangxi came to believe himself in danger, certain that Yinreng would try and avenge Songgotu's death. In late 1708, during the annual imperial hunting party at Mulan, Kangxi publicly deposed Yinreng as heir-apparent. "Since [Yinreng] must want to see the disintegration of my state and want to kill all my people, how can I make such a person the emperor? What would become of the empire I have inherited from my ancestors?"[2]

Less than a year later, Kangxi was prevailed upon by his officials to effect a reconciliation, but Yinreng's degenerate behavior resumed, and this time Kangxi showed more resolution. From then on, right to the end of his life, Kangxi was evasive over naming a new heir. He had thirty-six sons, twenty of whom grew to maturity; when Yinreng was dismissed, seven other sons emerged as serious contenders for the throne. It would not have been possible, given the political conditions of the time, to prevent factions forming around the contenders, and indeed much bitter rivalry and feuding among the princes over the question of succession marred the last years of Kangxi's reign.

In the end the victor was not the obvious choice. Kangxi's successor was Yongzheng, his fourth son. Yongzheng's mother, the daughter of a bodyguard, had been lowly born, and it was not until she had a son that the title Concubine of the Fourth Grade was bestowed on her.

Yongzheng succeeded his father amid insinuations that he had usurped the throne. He certainly had to suppress the threat posed by his disappointed brothers, several of whom were arrested and later died in prison. Nevertheless, there is a persuasive story that gives the credit of his ascendancy to his son Hongli, who was in time to ascend the throne as the great emperor Qianlong.

It was 1722; Kangxi, now sixty-nine years old, was ailing. The intrigues at court centered on the pretensions of his sons continued to cause him great anguish. One day, he was invited by his fourth son, the future Yongzheng emperor, to visit Yuanmingyuan.

Yuanmingyuan, the Garden of Perfect Brightness, was an estate northwest of the capital city. First landscaped by Kangxi and then given to his fourth son as a summer palace, Yuanmingyuan included a particularly fine Peony Terrace, where on this day Kangxi was entertained to food and wine and treated to a lovely view of the flowers in full bloom. In an expansive mood, Kangxi called for his grandchildren to join him.

The meeting of Kangxi and Hongli, who was after all merely one of Kangxi's 123 grandsons, was later described as fateful. Bright, confident and with a frank and penetrating gaze, young Hongli soon filled the empty place in Kangxi's heart.

A festive street in Nanjing, from the scroll recording Kangxi's southern tour.

It is said that Kangxi's fondness for the grandson enhanced the chances of succession by the father. There is even a belief that a secret understanding was reached between Kangxi and Yongzheng, for Yongzheng to succeed on condition that the favorite grandson would be in turn named heir-apparent.

Kangxi died in the sixty-first year of his reign, probably of heart failure. He had long prepared for death, and to the last he was punctilious in his ritual obligations. Between the time he fell ill and the day he died, he ordered his fourth son to offer sacrifices at the Temple of Heaven, and his fifth son to make obeisances at Dongling, the Eastern Tombs of the Qing emperors. The day after his death, his heir Yongzheng arranged for funeral rites to be held at the Palace of Heavenly Purity, where the coffin lay in state for twenty days. Then, following established practice, it was placed in a mourning hall on Prospect Hill behind the Forbidden City, and a wake was held with much burnt offering. Perhaps insecure about his claim to the throne, Yongzheng made a great show of filial piety, decreeing that, instead of wearing full mourning clothes for twenty-one days as was the custom, the court was to wear them for a hundred days. This was clearly impractical, as many occasions required the donning of special ceremonial robes, so the mourning clothes were left off after twenty-nine days.

Yongzheng then made another

pronouncement: since the Palace of Heavenly Purity had been Kangxi's main residence, he would not show disrespect to his father's

Yongzheng at leisure in Yuanmingyuan, the Garden of Perfect Brightness.

memory by presuming to live there himself. Thereafter Qing emperors lived in the Hall of Mental Cultivation. Again to demonstrate his filial piety, Yongzheng decided against cremation, which was the Manchu tradition, and Kangxi was buried instead. Yongzheng personally accompanied the funeral cortege to

the mausoleum in the Eastern Qing Tombs.

In 1735, after a brief reign, when Yongzheng himself departed on the distant journey to join his ancestors, a casket was reverently taken down from its hiding place behind the plaque in the Palace of Heavenly Purity. In it was a simple document nominating Hongli as the next emperor. Under his reign title of Qianlong, Hongli issued an edict explaining that Yongzheng had made no public choice of an heir, but in the first year of his reign he had written Hongli's name and placed it in a locked casket, which he had secreted at the back of the imperial plaque, *Zheng Da Guang Ming*. He also wrote the name on a piece of paper that he put in a pouch which he wore on his person. When the two pieces of paper were opened and the seal impressions compared, there was no doubt that the testament was genuine. The empire was then commanded to give Qianlong its allegiance.

Yongzheng had been determined that the bloody struggle between him and his brothers for the dragon throne would never be repeated. He established a custom that continued through the next three generations.

1 Jonathan D. Spence: *Emperor of China: Self-Portrait of K'ang-hsi*

2 Quoted in Silas H.L. Wu: *Passage to Power, K'ang-hsi and His Heir Apparent 1661-1722*

IMPERIAL TOURS

Painted on silk by Wang Hui and other artists of the imperial studio, the collection of twelve scrolls, *Emperor Kangxi's Tour of the South,* is a record of an expedition undertaken in 1689. Like a newsreel, nine of the scrolls document the entire journey south, beginning with Kangxi's departure from the Forbidden City and ending with his arrival at Shaoxing, a town south of the Yangzi

subjects in the faraway southern provinces, where many Ming loyalists still clung to the memory of the fallen dynasty. He was equally aware that showing his personal interest went some way toward improving the water control work on the major river systems of the country, particularly the Yangzi basin, a rich source of the tribute grains, silk and other commodities so necessary to the imperial household. He (and Qianlong after him) made an unusually large number of such tours.

Each one lasted several months and mobilized up to three thousand people, six thousand horses and a thousand boats. The emperor might be accompanied by members of his family, officials, guards, soldiers and retainers, and they all needed transport, temporary accommodation and feeding on the way. It was all immensely expensive, so it is not surprising to learn from one record that the cost at each stop was "ten to twenty thousand taels of silver" in Kangxi's day. By the time Qianlong was making them, the tours had become a burden on the state treasury.

River; the other three scrolls depict his return. Kangxi spent three months completing this tour; it was three years before his court painters put the last brush stroke on to their stupendous work.

Imperial tours had the obvious benefit of allowing the emperor to view, at first hand, the conditions under which his subjects lived, and conversely of letting the populace see with their own eyes the glorious progress of the Son of Heaven and his splendid entourage. Kangxi was particularly sensitive to the need to conciliate his

(Above) Kangxi's tour of the south. (Pages 92-93) Crossing the Yangzi during the tour.

THE SUN AT NOON

When the sun stands at midday, it begins to set; when the moon is full

it begins to wane. The fullness and emptiness of heaven and earth wane and wax in

the course of time. How much truer this is of men, or of spirits and gods!

Commentary on the fifty-fifth hexagram of *The Book of Changes,*

from Jonathan D. Spence: *The Search for Modern China*

THE ABUNDANCE OF QIANLONG

The emperor Qianlong's reign is often described as a period of stability and prosperity. China enjoyed peace at home and military victory abroad, and vast tracts of land — including today's Xinjiang Uygur Autonomous Region — were integrated, so that the empire doubled in size. A firm border with the Russians was agreed; the frontiers in the far southwest were secured; and Burma, Siam and Korea became suzerain states, which once a year sent tribute missions to the emperor.

It was the custom for tribute missions to bring the emperor ritual gifts. We know from a painting by the Jesuit court artist Giuseppe Castiglione that central Asian horses were presented to Qianlong by Kazaks from China's northwest frontier. Horses delighted Qianlong, for he had been trained in the traditional Manchu hunting skills in the great parks established by his grandfather Kangxi. Qianlong greatly expanded the imperial resort of Rehe (Jehol) — a favorite hunting ground located outside the Great Wall and close to Manchuria, the Qing emperors' ancestral home — where he built eight magnificent temples on the hills surrounding the palace. To integrate and, in some cases, to placate the rulers of the newly subjugated territories, Qianlong modeled

these temples on those of their religions and cultures: the Putuo Zongsheng Miao, for example, is a copy of the Potala in Lhasa. The court would move up to the cool of the resort during the hot summer months, which

(Page 94-95) Square in front of the Gate of Heavenly Purity. (Opposite) Accession portrait of emperor Qianlong. (Above) Engraving of Haiyan Hall in Yuanmingyan. (Pages 98-99) Troating for deer.

---

frequently coincided with the timing of the tribute missions.

Emulating another habit of his grandfather, Qianlong made elaborate expeditions around the empire, and particularly to the Yangzi valley. His mother would often accompany him on these trips. Both were entranced by the southern landscape, its green and watery paddy fields, its gentle hills and misty lakes and its towns graced by temples and pagodas — Yangzhou (on the Grand Canal northeast

of Nanjing) was a particular favorite. To remind his mother of these "grand tours" in her old age, Qianlong ordered a street in southern-style architecture to be built in the capital.

Qianlong was an enthusiastic patron of art and literature, and the imperial collection of books and paintings was greatly enlarged during his reign. The emperor himself was an accomplished calligrapher and poet, so that many temple inscriptions around China contain examples of his works. Under his direction most of the great classics of Chinese literature, as well as twenty-four dynastic histories, were compiled into *The Four Treasuries,* a massive anthology that boasts 3,450 complete works. (Sadly, however, the editors of the project were instructed to destroy anything considered critical of Manchu culture, and some two thousand works fell foul of their literary inquisition.)

Like Kangxi, Qianlong welcomed Jesuits to his court — but as astronomers, architects and painters, not as teachers of the Christian faith. The Jesuits had hoped that the new emperor would be more lenient than his predecessors, and were understandably devastated when he endorsed previous decrees forbidding them from spreading their religion. Qianlong, too, distrusted Christian-

(Pages 100-101) Battle scene during emperor Qianlong's campaigns to subjugate the western regions, by Castiglione and others. (Above) Handscroll of Qianlong receiving tribute horses from Kazaks, by Castiglione.

ity as a potential source of subversion. Nevertheless, he was happy to support the Jesuits' artistic endeavors, and the fathers were provided with a studio in the Forbidden City, where Qianlong visited them on an almost daily basis. Giuseppe Castiglione, perhaps the greatest of the Jesuit painters, records the intense frustration he felt: "Just imagine that I am considered well rewarded by seeing him [the emperor] every day . . . To be on a chain from one sun to the next; barely to have Sundays and feast days on which to pray to God; to paint almost nothing in keeping with one's own taste and genius; to have to put up with a thousand other harassments . . . It would quickly make me return to Europe if I did not believe my brush useful for the good of Religion and a means of making the Emperor favourable towards the missionaries who preach it."[1]

The Jesuits also designed great buildings for the Qianlong emperor, who called for "palaces in the manner of European barbarians in the midst of a multitude of jets of water, cascades and fountains."[2] The resulting extravagant pleasure houses, built in the baroque style and set around fountains similar to those at Versailles, stood beside the summer palace of Yuanmingyuan, some six miles to the northwest of the Forbidden City.

Castiglione designed the Italianate buildings while another Jesuit employed in the court, Michel Benoist, constructed the mechanical fountains.

A conscientious albeit traditionalist ruler, Qianlong was nevertheless unable to prevent the gradual weakening of the empire during the last two decades of his reign. His military campaigns, grand tours and architectural projects were enormously expensive, and placed an excessive pressure on the state's finances. Corruption was also growing —

officials in the provinces often managed to keep surplus tax revenues for themselves — and this waning of central control was combined with an inability to understand the demands of Western commerce impatient for access to the massive potential of the Celestial Kingdom. The China of Qianlong kept aloof from the world behind a cultural and economic wall built on the belief of its own superiority and self-sufficiency. Qianlong, presiding over the empire's golden afternoon, remained magnificently unaware that Europe

had made dramatic strides in the development of technology and science, overtaking China in industrial production, or that world trade had become increasingly dominated by Great Britain.

1   Cécile and Michel Beurdeley: *Giuseppe Castiglione*
2   *Giuseppe Castiglione*

IMPERIAL PLEASANCES

MAGGIE KESWICK

Gardening, like painting and ceramics, is one of the great arts of China. There are four gardens in the Forbidden City, of which two are open to the public. The Imperial Garden, laid out in emperor Yongle's time, located at the northern end of the palace complex, is the largest and oldest. The other, commonly known as Qianlong's Garden, lies in the northeast corner, together with the Palace of Peaceful Longevity. It was to this quiet retreat that the emperor Qianlong ostensibly retired on New Year's day in 1796, after sixty years on the throne. Formally he abdicated out of filial respect for his grandfather, the emperor Kangxi, who had ruled sixty-one years, but in practice he barely relinquished power and his successor, his fifteenth son Jiaqing (reigned 1796-1820), ruled only in name until Qianlong's death in 1799.

Like other Chinese gardens, the ones in the Forbidden City were designed to create a microcosm of *shanshui* (the Chinese name for "landscape" which literally translates as mountains and water), and to evoke a range of effects and emotions that might be experienced traveling in the wilderness. European palaces are usually set in huge parks; the Imperial Garden and Qianlong's Garden are *internal* gardens — and to suggest in such tight spaces all the variety of nature requires extraordinary ingenuity. In the famous gardens of southern China, the garden-makers designed labyrinths in which the available space is layered by gateways and subdivided by walls. Each garden becomes a composition of enclosed spaces, all of them full of incident — pools, bridges, halls, pavilions perched on giant rockeries, libraries, galleries, terraces, pathways floored with pebble mosaics (there are charming pebble pictures of a bicycle and motor cars in the Imperial Garden).

Typically, the garden is as much concerned with architecture as with growing things, but with a lyrical spontaneity and freshness of design rather different from the more formal arrangements of trees and pavilions in Beijing.

Within the Forbidden City, the Imperial Garden takes on the careful symmetry of the Palace itself, each tree on the left with its counterpart on the right, each pavilion with its fellow balancing it on the other side. The Hall of Imperial Peace (Qinandian), a Taoist shrine at the center of the garden and the most intact Ming building in the palace complex, is flanked by the Pavilion of A Thousand Autumns on the west and the Pavilion of Ten Thousand Springs on the east. A pair of identical bronze *qilins*, mythical beasts similar to unicorns, guard the First Gate of Heaven in front of Qinandian, and bamboo groves are placed symmetrically each side.

The garden, however, also holds a collection of strange, rare and oddly shaped rocks, placed singly on pedestals like pieces of sculpture. Some are semi-precious stones, others natural curiosities, still others soft limestone hollowed by water and time, pitted with holes and seemingly frozen in perpetual motion — and regarded as aesthetic objects in their own right. The less individually distinctive stones are piled up into hugh artificial "mountains," like the one known as the Hill of Accumulated Elegance, its peak crowned with a swoop-eaved pavilion to which the courtiers would ascend every year on the ninth of September, in keeping with the custom of climbing hills on the festival of Chongyang. All of these bring an element of strangeness — of "otherness" into the tight formal

(Opposite) The imperial resort of Rehe, by Leng Mei.

spaces of the courtyards — but none so much as the garden's ancient and beautiful juniper trees, their trunks gnarled and gouged in patterns reminiscent of the turbulent waters of a river rapid. High above the tourists and citizens, their topmost branches feather out in a soft, sighing canopy of needles against the brilliant northern sky, shading the sheltered terraces below.

Qianlong's Garden occupies an even smaller space; it is nevertheless full of pavilions with complex latticework windows giving surprising vistas of a gnarled tree or a corner of brilliantly painted eaves. It too contains many arrangements of intricate rockeries. Other features reflect the idea of the garden as a place for contemplation and the most appropriate and inspiring place in which to paint or write poetry. In the southwest corner, the Pavilion of Ceremonial Purification (Xishangting) includes a "cup-floating stream" cut into the paving of its open-sided porch — a device for a light-hearted poetry-rhyming game in which each participant must compose a line more quickly than it takes a wine-cup to float down the winding stream toward him. The forfeit for failing was to drink in one draft the wine in the cup so, as the game progressed, the losers grew less and less capable of finishing their lines — and merrier and merrier.

The Chinese garden was a retreat in many senses, a place to relax with wine and friends. Painting or fine calligraphy, listening to music, looking at antiques and perhaps a little amorous dalliance were all pleasures of the garden. But above all they were places where a person could tune himself to the rhythms of the natural world by celebrating seasonal changes: plum blossom on bare winter branches; the scent of lotus on the summer evening breeze;

chrysanthemums in autumn; the moon reflected in a dark pool.

When Qianlong felt an urge to build gardens, he argued that a retreat was essential for his moral health: "Every emperor and ruler, when he has retired from audience, and has finished his public duties, must have a garden in which he may stroll, look around and relax his heart. If he has a suitable place for this it will refresh his mind and regulate his emotions, but if he has not, he will become engrossed in sensual pleasures and lose his will power."

It sounds fair enough, but of course it contains a paradox: for wise and conscientious rulers, a garden is an essential place of spiritual rejuvenation, yet its very loveliness can also be a temptation to sensual excess. For Qianlong it was both — not that he was a weak monarch, or unconcerned with his duties, but because he was swept away with a passion for the beauties of nature and with the desire to create beautiful places. At the same time he was acutely conscious of the frugal example left him by his grandfather, Kangxi, in whose lovely, but quite modest garden, he had lived as a child.

When he first came to the throne, Qianlong was torn between the longing to landscape on a wider scale and the very serious desire not to "bring shame upon myself and my ancestors" by any form of excess. With what was clearly a Herculean effort of will, he held back for three years during the period of mourning for his father's death, continuing to live modestly in his previous apartments and manfully rejecting all the court eunuchs' suggestions for building.

But the little courtyard gardens of the Palace were, simply, not enough and eventually, in the grounds of his father's summer palace outside the capital, a thousand workmen could be seen forming hills and valleys and lakes and winding canals, with all the pavilions, bridges and rockeries appropriate for an imperial retreat equal to the most lavish in history. This garden — the Garden of Perfect Brightness or Yuanmingyuan — included a landscape of "nature improved," lavish pavilions, great halls for entertainments and audiences, and tiny corners for study. In addition the emperor built in it a vast library to house one complete set of the great Qing collection of classical works. There were also temples, the complete reproduction of a southern city street and of rustic farms, drill grounds for training troops and, as the artist-missionary, Father Jean-Denis Attiret, noted, "little parks for the chase" — although, judging

---

(Opposite) Watching opera was also one of the pleasures of the garden; this stage is in the Lodge for Retired Life (Juanqinzhai) in Qianlong's Garden. (Below) "Cup-floating stream."

by the plans of the garden, any hunts staged there must have been on a very small scale. Inevitably the garden also contained an immense collection of different plants and many small menageries in which interesting or unusual beasts were kept. Most extraordinary of all — and this was certainly an innovation — were a series of buildings in carved stonework occupying the northeast boundary of Yuanmingyuan. Here Qianlong commissioned the Jesuits he employed in his court to build him a collection of halls with fountains and a maze in imitation of European baroque — a kind of reverse Chinoiserie. Of all the treasures of Yuanmingyuan, the ruins of these are all that remain today.

In Chinese folk tales a connection was sometimes made between the growth of imperial luxury and the decline of great dynasties. As often as not the symbols of such luxury have been beautiful women and imperial parks. It is a connection confirmed by history. The end of dynasties has almost inevitably been accompanied by the shrieks of women, the crash of falling rockeries and the crackle of burning pavilions. Thus, when on the morning of October 18, 1860, a great pall of smoke rose up over the towers of Yuanmingyuan and began to drift slowly eastward, dropping splinters of burning wood, hot ash and cinders into the courtyards and *hutongs* of Beijing, it was in many ways a well-established confirmation that the Qing dynasty was nearing its end.

Some years after the destruction, a Chinese minister to London reassessed the loss, and added to the traditional moral a new awareness of China's place in the world. For him the burning signified his country's awakening: "By the light of the burning palaces which had been the delight of her emperors, [China] commenced to see that she had been asleep while all the world was up and doing . . . The Summer Palace with all its wealth of art was a high price to pay for the lesson we there received, but not too high, if it has taught us to repair and triply fortify our battered armor: — and it has done so."

Perhaps he was right in the long run, yet there would be another extravagant summer palace built before the last dynasty ran its course — the Garden for Cultivating Harmony of the empress dowager Cixi. Part of a substantial loan raised to equip and modernize a Chinese navy was appropriated for the building. Thus when China needed a navy to fight against Japan, she did not have an effective one available. Despite the examples of imperial indulgence, though, the Chinese always seem to have kept an alternative set of values with which to judge their emperors' works. It is of course a Taoist alternative, here expressed by an old gardener as he looked across at the tile roofs of Cixi's summer palace glimmering in the sun: "Many people nowadays blame the empress for using the money to build a garden instead of buying warships to fight with foreign countries. But I think she did a wise thing. War is a beastly idea after all. Look! . . . Who would ever have thought that such beautiful things could be made by the hands of men, had she not spent the money on it?"

Part of this material first appeared in Maggie Keswick: *The Chinese Garden*

(Opposite) Pavilions of Qianlong's Garden.

EAST MEETS WEST

In 1792, when Qianlong was eighty-two years old, King George III of Great Britain sent George Lord Macartney as Ambassador Extraordinary and Plenipotentiary to the emperor of China. Macartney was charged with the tasks of negotiating a commercial treaty to open China up to British trade and pressing for permission to establish a British diplomatic presence in Beijing.

By the end of the eighteenth century, an active triangular trade had developed in tea, silk, rhubarb and porcelain from China; woolens, metals and knick-knacks from Britain; and raw cotton, sandalwood, silver and opium from India. But, under Chinese law, foreign merchants were confined to the southern port of Canton (Guangzhou), and they could transact business only through thirteen authorized Chinese agents known as *hongs*. These restrictions made trade difficult and profit margins small. More than twenty million pounds of tea were being shipped from China to Britain annually, and the silver bullion used to pay for sustaining the British fashion for tea-drinking tipped the balance of trade very much in China's favor. It was in the hope of redressing this situation by direct appeal to the emperor of China that the embassy was launched.

Although the East India Company footed much of the bill, Britain was sufficiently aware of the mission's importance to ensure that its personnel were of the highest caliber. Macartney himself has been described as an

(Opposite) Qianlong on horseback, by Castiglione. (Above) Lord Macartney.

intelligent and attractive personality, an excellent conversationalist and a good linguist. His interest in China had apparently been fueled by his friendship with Voltaire, whom he met in Paris soon after the publication of *Orphelia de la Chine,* Voltaire's eulogy on the Celestial Kingdom. In 1764, at the age of twenty-seven, he had been dispatched

as Envoy Extraordinary to the court of Catherine the Great for two years; he had subsequently held the post of governor in the Caribbean and then India.

Joining Macartney on his embassy to China were Sir George Staunton as deputy and official diarist, as well as scholars, geographers, painters, physicians and, of course, diplomats. In all, seven hundred men boarded the *Lion,* the *Hindostan* and the *Jackall* in Portsmouth harbor on September 26, 1792.

Ten months later Macartney's flotilla dropped anchor at the mouth of the Beihe River on the northeast coast of China. From this moment on difficulties of protocol, face and misunderstanding stalked the mission. Waiting to greet Macartney were two officials. Wang Wenxiong, a military officer of the second grade who "was a true character of his profession, open, bold and brave . . Beside a red globe above his bonnet, he was honoured with another mark of favour for his services. This was literally a feather, and taken from a peacock's tail. He was cheerful and pleasant . . . treating his new friends with the familiarity of old acquaintance."[1] His companion Qiao Renjie was "a man of grave, but not austere manners . . . considered a man of learning and judgement. He

Porcelain manufacturing in China was well developed during the Qing. Tea, silk and china made up the bulk of the cargoes being shipped to Europe from Canton.

bore the honorary distinction of a blue globe [official of the third rank] placed upon the bonnet covering his head." They were accompanied by the Manchu Zheng Rui, an official of higher rank. Wang and Qiao actually made the difficult journey on to the *Lion;* she was so high out of the water that they had to be hauled up by a pulley. Zheng Rui, however, did not attempt to board the ship. Where the British were concerned, this refusal signified the legate's haughty disposition and fear of the sea. But, according to the imperial archives, the *Lion* had stood higher in the water than the Chinese officials' junk, and it was unseemly for the emperor's representative to go *up* a gangplank to greet an emissary from a tributary state.

Macartney had arrived in a country which had no department of foreign affairs. Relations with states on China's borders, such as Burma and Korea, were traditionally conducted on a footing which reflected China's cultural and political superiority. These states paid tribute to China, and not only their emissaries but also their rulers would kowtow to the Chinese emperor. Although Macartney had been instructed in London to conform to the protocol of the Chinese court, he balked at prostrating himself and knocking his forehead on the ground; he felt that such an act would undermine the dignity of his country.

By August 5 the embassy had begun the journey upriver on three brigs of the fleet,

with the servants, guards, musicians and gifts for the emperor following on board junks — above which fluttered a flag with Chinese characters which stood for "tribute embassy of red barbarians." Macartney was aware of the slight but chose to ignore it.

The dreaded matter of the kowtow arose soon enough; as the mission journeyed toward Beijing the subject was raised several times. Wang and Qiao actually offered to teach Macartney the kowtow, while Zheng Rui suggested that the problem could merely be one of clothing. The foreigners' tight breeches and garters might make it physically impossible for them to kneel, in which case all that was needed was a temporary removal of those garments.

The presents for Qianlong became another source of misunderstanding between East and West. Enormous trouble had been taken in selecting what were thought to be suitable gifts for the emperor of China. Representing the summit of eighteenth-century technology, these gifts included clocks, guns, telescopes, a planetarium and even an orrery (a clockwork solar system), an impressive collection worth £13,124. Fearful that the larger, more delicate objects would be damaged if they were hauled across dirt tracks enroute to Rehe, where the emperor was spending the summer and the audience was to take place, Macartney requested that they be stored in Beijing to await Qianlong's return. After much negotiation Zheng Rui

agreed, although he was amazed at the foreigners' stupidity: it was customary for an embassy to deposit all its gifts at the emperor's feet — not to do so simply demeaned the mission.

On their arrival in Beijing, Staunton records how unlike European cities the Chinese capital was: "Here few houses were higher than one story; none more than two; while the width of the street which divided them was considerably above one hundred feet. It was airy, gay, and lightsome." As they were driven through the city the visitors caught their first sight of the Forbidden City: "A halt was made opposite the treble gates which are nearly in the centre of this northern side of the palace wall. It appeared to inclose a large quantity of ground . . . on the hills of different heights the principal palaces for the Emperor were erected. The whole had somewhat the appearance of enchantment." The observant travelers noted that the feet of the Tartar (Manchu) women "free from bandages . . . were suffered to attain their natural growth,"[2] while Chinese women, conforming to the convention and fashion of the day, had bound feet. The British made their way through the city to the northwest until they reached their lodging in Yuanmingyuan, where the presents were unpacked and laid out in one of the halls. To Macartney's satisfaction they provided "an assemblage of such beauty . . . not to be seen collected together in any other apartment, I believe, in the whole world besides."

During their sojourn at Yuanmingyuan, Macartney wrote a memorial clarifying how he would deal with the ceremonials at the imperial audience, but so controversial was this paper deemed to be that initially no one would translate it for him. Eventually Staunton's twelve-year-old son, who was traveling as the ambassador's page and had managed to pick up sufficient Chinese to be able to copy characters, managed to inscribe the letter. The suggestion in the letter which had so horrified the Chinese was that Macartney would perform a full kowtow as long as an official of similar rank would perform the same ritual in front of a portrait of King George. They simply could not understand why such an issue was being made of it. Eventually a way was found to satisfy everyone. Macartney would kneel on one knee in front of Qianlong as he would to his own king, though the kissing of the imperial hand — a Western custom — was dispensed with.

At the beginning of September the embassy left for Rehe, Macartney traveling in his English post-chaise, "the first piece of Long Acre manufactory that ever rattled along the road to Jehol."[3] On arrival, Macartney's memorial was placed in the hands of Heshen, one of the six members of the Grand Council and reputedly the most powerful man in China — and also, it was rumored, Qianlong's lover. The hoped-for audience finally took place at dawn on September 14, in an imposing Mongolian yurt in the grounds of Rehe. "Soon after day-light," wrote Staunton, "the sound of several instruments, and the confused voices of men at a distance, announced the Emperor's approach. He was clad in plain dark silk, with a velvet bonnet."

"The Embassador . . . held the large and magnificent square box of gold, adorned with jewels, in which was inclosed his Majesty's letter to the Emperor, between both hands lifted above his head; and in that manner ascending the few steps that led to the throne, and bending on one knee, presented the box with a short address, to his Imperial Majesty; who, graciously receiving the same with his own hands, placed it by his side, and expressed 'the satisfaction he felt at the testimony which his Britannic Majesty gave to him of his esteem and good will, in sending him an Embassy, with a letter, and rare presents; that he, on his part, entertained sentiments of the same kind towards the sovereign of Great Britain, and hoped that harmony should always be maintained among their respective subjects.' . . . His Imperial Majesty, after a little more conversation with the Embassador, gave, as the first present from him to his Majesty, a gem . . . It was upwards of a foot in length, and curiously carved into a form intended to resemble a sceptre, such as is always placed upon the Imperial throne, and is considered as emblematic of prosperity and peace."

Emperor Qianlong's edict to George III, written in Chinese, Latin and Manchu scripts. (Pages 116-17) Rear view of the foreign trade area in Canton.

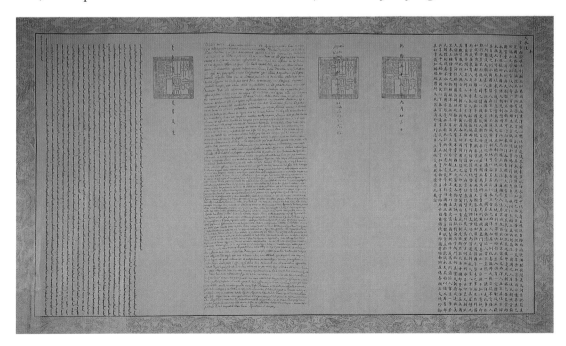

Later Qianlong, discovering the young pageboy Staunton's proficiency in Chinese, presented him with a purse. A banquet followed during which the emperor sent his European guests "several dishes from his own table; and, when it was over, he sent for them; and presented with his own hands to them, a goblet of warm Chinese wine, not unlike Madeira of an inferior quality. He asked the Embassador the age of his own sovereign; of which being informed, he immediately replied, that he heartily wished him to equal himself in years, which already amounted to eighty three, and with as perfect health. He was indeed yet so hale and vigorous, that he scarcely appeared to have existed as many years, fifty-seven, as in fact, he had governed the empire. When the festival was entirely over, and he descended from his throne, he marched firm and erect, and without the least symptom of infirmity, to the open chair that was waiting for him."

The pomp and grandeur of Qianlong's court moved Macartney to record in his own journal: "Thus I have seen Solomon in all his glory." Discussing the business at hand, however, proved to be impossible at that first meeting, as it did during subsequent encounters with the emperor or with the powerful Heshen who, Macartney noted, was particularly adept at steering the conversation away from serious matters.

On September 21 the embassy was

Emperor Qianlong arriving for audience with Lord Macartney at Rehe.

required to leave Rehe and journey back to Beijing, where the British were to await the emperor's return. The contents of George III's letter had dismayed the emperor, who was now convinced that the barbarians had been sent to spy on the court: he had no intention of agreeing to a British representative being stationed in Beijing. Within a fortnight, Heshen had summoned Macartney to a meeting and announced that the court was worried about Macartney's health — indeed he was suffering from bad rheumatism and many of his staff had dysentery — and that the British should leave for home before the winter set in. Dismayed at his dismissal, Macartney reminded Heshen of the promise he had made in Rehe to discuss the various objectives of his mission.

The early morning of October 3 saw Macartney rise from his sickbed, don his ceremonial clothes and travel to the Forbidden City for the first and only time. "The palace is encompassed by a high wall," wrote Staunton, "within which he was conducted through spacious courts, along canals of stagnant water, and over bridges of granite, with balustrades of marble, to the foot of the hall, where he found the Emperor's answer contained in a large roll covered in yellow silk, and placed on a chair of state hung with curtains of the same colour." Macartney and his suite mounted the steps to the Hall of Supreme Harmony, "a single structure surrounded by many others, itself of great size and magnificence, tho' built of wood upon a foundation of granite, and decorated within side and out, with gilding, and in the happiest disposition of the most pleasing and vivid colours."

Macartney left the Forbidden City knowing his embassy to have been a complete failure. He had not been able to engage in any substantive negotiations regarding the purposes for which he had traveled half way round the world; he had not been permitted to establish a permanent mission in Beijing; he had achieved nothing on behalf of the merchants in Canton. The emperor, meanwhile, remained secure in his conviction that his realm was the center of the world and that it had little need of outside trade. In his edict to George III, Qianlong declared: " . . .We have never valued ingenious articles, nor do we have the slightest need of your country's manufactures. Therefore, O King, as regards your request to send someone to remain at the capital, while it is not in harmony with the regulations of the Celestial Empire, we also feel very much that it is of no advantage to your country. Hence we have commanded your tribute envoys to return safely home. You, O King, should simply act in conformity with our wishes by strengthening your loyalty and swearing perpetual obedience so as to ensure that your country may share the blessings of peace."[4]

Macartney was, however, able to retain a sense of perspective, and on his return to England he wrote prophetically of the Qing dynasty's collapse: "The Empire of China is an old, crazy, first-rate Man of War, which a fortunate succession of able and vigilant officers have contrived to keep afloat for these hundred and fifty years past, and to over-awe their neighbours merely by her bulk and appearance. But, whenever an insufficient man happens to have command on deck, adieu to the discipline and safety of the ship. She may, perhaps, not sink outright; she may drift some time as a wreck, and will then be dashed to pieces on the shore; but she can never be rebuilt on the old bottom."[5] Indeed, as Macartney feared, there were no able and vigilant officers to command the Chinese man-of-war after Qianlong. The mission, though a failure in its time, turned out to be the first indication of the great historical forces which would sweep away the whole imperial system by the next century. The doors to China's trade were then finally opened — and by force of arms rather than by diplomacy.

1   And all other unattributed quotations from Sir George Staunton: *Macartney's Embassy to China*
2   Aeneas Anderson: *A Narrative of the British Embassy to China*
3   Maurice Collis: *The Great Within*
4   Quoted from Alain Peyrefitte: *The Collision of Two Civilisations*
5   Quoted in J.L. Cranmer-Byng, "Lord Macartney's Embassy to Peking in 1793," *Journal of Oriental Studies IV (1967-68)*

WALLS OF THE MIND

As Qianlong's reign drew to a close, the wheel of dynastic fortune turned. The dawn of the new century, a year after the death of Qianlong, found his son Jiaqing as emperor; his favorite and outrageously corrupt grand councilor Heshen at last exposed and stripped of his vast fortune, waiting to carry out the "order" to commit suicide; a group of anti-Qing rebels called the White Lotus Sect making inroads in the southern provinces, though the central government refused to recognize the threat; and the opium problem totally out of hand.

The first shipment of two hundred chests of opium (each containing between 130 and 160 pounds) had arrived in Canton in 1729. Determined to find a satisfactory cargo for the empty ships sailing from India to China, where they loaded up with tea, the East India Company had secured a monopoly on the production of Indian opium. The thick, processed paste was then shipped by selected merchants to Canton, but never in the Company's own ships, which were prohibited from carrying the so-called "foreign mud." On arrival in Chinese waters the drug would be transferred to huge barges lying offshore; then, at dead of night, sampans manned by teams of strong, fast rowers would offload the cargo.

Within a year of the first shipment docking at Canton the emperor Yongzheng had banned the smoking of opium except for medicinal purposes — it was said to be good

(Opposite) Gilded handle on a Palace door.
(Above) The ruins of Yuanmingyuan.

for diarrhea and fever (as well as being an aphrodisiac). The penalty if caught indulging in the habit was a month of wearing the cangue; for distributing the drug, strangulation. Nonetheless, by the turn of the century trade had increased to around 4,570 cases per annum and opium was smoked by all strata of Chinese society — eunuchs of the court; society ladies imprisoned within their own demesne (and immobilized by their bound "lily feet"); guests relaxing over a pipe after dinner; businessmen who felt the need of courage; and soldiers for some added strength. It has been suggested that unscrupulous employers would supply opium tablets to their coolies to enable them to carry still heavier loads. Some historians also assert that members of the Chinese literati took the drug to alleviate the shame and frustration of living life under the Manchus.

In 1800 opium was banned for any purposes at all. This was to little effect, however: between 1820 and 1830 annual imports rose to more than ten thousand chests, while prices dropped. The British merchant William Jardine was quite candid in a letter dated 1832: "Our principal reliance is on opium . . by many considered an immoral traffic, yet such traffic is . . . absolutely necessary to give any vessel a reasonable chance of defraying expenses."[1] Alarm bells sounded in the Forbidden City, and emperor Daoguang (reigned 1821-50) realized that even firmer action had to be taken. What was more, the balance of trade had by now been reversed, with silver flowing from the Chinese coffers at a sufficient rate to cause an economic crisis.

In January 1838 Daoguang appointed an

Opium den.

official named Lin Zexu, former governor-general of Hubei and Hunan, as special commissioner to deal with the opium question, equipping him with an imperial seal which conferred unprecedented powers upon him. Commissioner Lin quickly shook up the Canton community, and by July he had confiscated 45,000 pounds of opium and 70,500 pipes and had arrested 1,600 smokers. As regards the suppliers, Lin wrote a very reasoned letter to Queen Victoria: "We have heard that in your honourable nation too, the people are not permitted to smoke the drug . . . In order to remove the source of evil thoroughly, would it not be better to prohibit its sale and manufacture rather than merely prohibit its consumption?"[2] He then appealed to the merchants themselves, requesting that they hand over the stored chests of opium so that they could be destroyed, as well as sign pledges promising to cease trading. When the merchants did not agree — claiming that as the opium was on consignment to them, they were not empowered to hand it over — the commis-

sioner blockaded Canton. Six difficult weeks later the merchants conceded, and watched as the contents of twenty thousand chests were mixed with lime and salt and flushed into the sea.

No pledges were signed, however. Instead, incensed by the destruction of their opium, the merchants called on support from home. A British naval squadron of sixteen warships carrying some four thousand men was mobilized, and the first vessel sailed into the Pearl River delta in October 1839. So began the Opium War, " . . . a war more unjust in its origin, a war calculated in its progress to cover this country with permanent disgrace, I do not know and have not read of," according to William Gladstone (who was to become prime minister in

1868), speaking in the British Parliament in 1840. He also noted in his diary: "I am in dread of the judgement of God upon England for our national iniquity towards China."[3] The war was humiliating for China as well — it brought to light the weakness and decay that had begun to eat away the glorious rule of the Qing at the end of Qianlong's reign.

By 1842 the war was over. Daoguang had to concede to the superior firepower of the British gunboats. In fact, China had fought with virtually no navy, and her men had

(Below) Watercolor of English fleet attacking Chinese vessels near Canton, by Admiral Sir William Robert Kennedy. (Right) Signing of the Treaty of Tianjin.

been hopelessly ill equipped (legend has it that the Chinese soldiers had to construct arms in the field from instruction books printed two centuries earlier). The Treaty of Nanjing, signed at the end of the war, was a milestone in Chinese history: now there could be no turning back the relentless advance of Western influence into China. Its main terms required China to pay $21 million in indemnities; to allow the ports of Canton (today's Guangzhou), Amoy (Xiamen), Foochow (Fuzhou), Ningpo (Ningbo) and Shanghai to be opened to foreign merchants and their families; and to cede the island of Hong Kong to Britain in perpetuity. The British also tried to negotiate the legalization of the opium trade, but on this point the emperor would not yield. This

and subsequent treaties over the next few years, which included rights of trade for France and America, imposed near-colonial status on large parts of coastal China and the Yangzi valley. According to one Chinese diplomat and historian: "The fundamental reason for the defeat in the Opium War was our backwardness. Our troops and armaments were anachronisms, our government was medieval, and our people, including the official class, had a medieval mentality. Although we risked our lives resisting, we were finally defeated. There was no mystery in our defeat; it was inevitable."[4]

Domestic turbulence was also rife. Four major disturbances erupted during the next twenty years; the most disruptive, the Taiping rebellion, claimed twenty million

lives. In the Forbidden City the court turned ever inward; it hastily built walls in the mind, its only weapon against threatening change being retreat behind time-honored traditions and rituals. It was into this world of make-believe that Cixi, a seventeen-year-old Manchu girl from Anhui in the south, entered as a concubine of the fifth grade to the newly enthroned emperor Xianfeng.

China's suspicions of the outside world increased. The Western powers, on the other hand, still found trading conditions irksome. The year 1858 saw the signing of a new agreement, the Treaty of Tianjin, which granted foreigners further concessions. While opium was not legalized, the terms regarding its import clearly flouted China's own law banning its sale and consumption. The agreement also provided for the long-requested resident British minister in Beijing, but in the event this proved of little avail as the new envoy, Frederick Bruce, found his way to the capital barred. Finally, in 1860, the West decided to press its demands once again by force, and Lord Elgin, at the head of a French and British force, marched on Beijing and the Forbidden City. Elgin claimed that the action was justified, as the failure to observe the treaty "releases us from any obligation to restrict our advance."[5]

The news that the French and British had successfully taken the Dagu Forts, thus opening up the route to Beijing, was at first greeted dismissively by Xianfeng. But when

negotiations failed and the allies continued their march toward the Forbidden City, the imperial chests were packed for flight to the safety of Rehe.

In the short time Cixi had basked in imperial favor, the young concubine became tainted with Xianfeng's fear and hatred of foreigners; she also acquired a taste for political power. Like Xianfeng's other advisers, Cixi was horrified by the emperor's cowardice. Meanwhile, memorials flooded in urging the emperor not to abandon the Forbidden City. One bold memorial went to the heart of the matter, asking Xianfeng if he would cast away the inheritance of his ancestors like a damaged shoe, and indeed what would history say of His Majesty for a thousand years to come?

By September 22 Elgin and the allies were on the outskirts of Beijing and Xianfeng could bear it no longer: that morning a caravan slipped through the gates of the Forbidden City, carrying the emperor, a furious Cixi with her infant son (Xianfeng's only boy child) and the court retinue. A short statement informed Elgin that the emperor was obliged by law to hunt in the autumn. Left behind to deal with the allies was Prince Gong, the emperor's half-brother — but others, realizing that the

emperor had abandoned the Forbidden City, soon followed suit.

After intense negotiations, the west gate of the empty city was opened on October

Empress dowager Cixi, by Hubert Vos.

13, with Elgin making his grand entrance a few days later. The Convention of Beijing ratified all the clauses of the Treaty of Tianjin: at last foreign representatives would

be stationed in the Chinese capital. In addition, the crumbling dynasty was forced to pay the allies a huge indemnity of eight million taels. At one point, as revenge for some lives lost, Elgin considered destroying the Forbidden City, but discovering that the exquisite summer palace of Yuanmingyuan was already being looted by French and British troops, ordered that to be razed instead. A certain Reverend M'Ghee lamented: "A pang of sorrow seizes on you, no eye will ever again gaze upon those buildings. You have seen them once and for all . . . Man cannot reproduce them."[6]

The closed gates now well and truly battered down, the Forbidden City was suddenly exposed to the inquisitive gaze of nineteenth-century Europe. It also inherited a new emperor, for Xianfeng died at Rehe shortly after the signing of the Convention of Beijing, and Cixi's son ascended the dragon throne as the Tongzhi emperor at the age of five. In a swift move that showed her skill at intrigue, Cixi managed to have herself proclaimed co-regent with Xianfeng's senior wife. The two dowagers then became quite literally the power behind the throne, for they attended all audiences sitting discreetly behind a yellow silk curtain — a procedure enacted to keep up the appearance of propriety and known as "Listening Behind Screens to Reports on Government Affairs."

Some reforms were introduced to help the Qing adapt to the foreigners in their midst. An Irishman, Robert Hart (affectionately known by officials as "our Hart"), was appointed inspector general of the Imperial Maritime Customs to ensure that duties were collected efficiently. The Zongli Yamen, the equivalent of a ministry of foreign affairs, was established under the direction of Prince Gong, the young emperor's uncle. But, despite these attempts at liberalization by forward-looking members of the court, the empress dowager was highly conservative on policy matters and passionate about preserving the power of the Qing.

Young Tongzhi grew up in a hot-house of intrigue and at a young age fell into a lifestyle of general debauchery. In the company of several eunuchs, he would slip out of the Forbidden City, "through an opening specially cut in the wall, to idle in 'Flower Streets and Willow Lanes'. A eunuch's cart, drawn by a fast pacing mule, would await him there, and it became a matter of common gossip that the Son of Heaven was frequently mixed up in drunken and disreputable brawls and would return to the throne, even after he had attained his majority, long past the hours fixed for audiences."[7] These nights of carousing soon caught up with the emperor who, his health weakened, died at the age of eighteen from smallpox.

Determined to retain her hold on power, Cixi contrived for her four-year-old nephew to fill the empty throne as emperor Guangxu, with herself again as co-regent. At dead of night a carriage — the soldiers' shoes and horses' hooves wrapped in straw so that the noise would not alert people to the news of Tongzhi's death — was dispatched to bring the child to the Forbidden City. Guangxu's succession was against dynastic law: because the new emperor was of the same generation as his predecessor, he was not a "descendant" who could properly participate in the rites of ancestor worship due to Tongzhi's memory. But no one dared to challenge Cixi when she protested that Guangxu would promptly be succeeded by an heir if he produced one.

Thus Cixi ensured another term of absolute power for herself, until Guangxu reached the age of eighteen, when she could no longer put off her retirement from government. In 1889 she finally had to remove herself to the Garden for Cultivating Harmony, her new summer palace. Then, out of the fevered atmosphere of an increasingly corrupt and decadent court, Guangxu stepped briefly into the spotlight. In 1898 the young emperor launched the Hundred Days' Reforms, a program of educational and anti-corruption measures designed to modernize the country. However, these attempts at reform had come too late, and Cixi was in any case quite opposed to them. Again she acted swiftly, returning to the Forbidden City and putting Guangxu under surveillance and detention. But the imperial house of Qing could offer little resistance to the increasingly dominant and powerful foreigners. An alienated populace once more rose in rebellion. Led by an anti-foreign group called the Boxers, this violent revolt clearly foreshadowed the imminent lapse of the Mandate of Heaven.

Guangxu and Cixi died within a day of each other, a coincidence that aroused suspicion of foul play. The empress dowager had the last say, nevertheless. On her deathbed, she decreed that the next emperor would be three-year-old Puyi, the childless Guangxu's nephew. He was destined to be the last of the line.

1   Quoted in Jack Beeching: *The Chinese Opium Wars*

2   Chang Hsin-pao: *Commissioner Lin and the Opium War*

3   *The Chinese Opium Wars*

4   Tsiang Ting-fu: *Modern Chinese History,* reprinted in Franz Shurman and Orville Schell (eds.), *China Readings 1: Imperial China*

5   H.B. Morse: *The Chronicles of the East India Company: Trading to China 1635-1834*

6   R.J.L. M'Ghee: *How We Got to Peking: A Narrative of the Campaign in China of 1860*

7. Juliet Bredon: *Peking*

THE BOXER REBELLION

"Revive the Qing, destroy the foreigner!" was the battle cry of the Boxers United in Righteousness, a secret society formed during the latter part of the nineteenth century in Shandong province, and dedicated to the extermination of all foreigners and Chinese converts to Christianity. This strange band of men and women, the majority of whom were peasants, believed that, by participating in pseudo-mystical rituals, they could make themselves invulnerable to the bullets of foreigners. Initiation ceremonies were performed in a Buddhist temple: a new recruit, decked out in bright colors, would face the southwest, genuflect, stamp on a cross and then fall into a trance. Once "possessed" the recruit was thought to be immune to all physical harm. Gatherings to display these powers were popular, so that soon the movement had a large membership — though strangely enough, it never had a leader.

With the decline of the Qing dynasty and the steady incursions of foreign influence, the life of the Chinese peasant had gradually become harder. The Boxers, however, suddenly provided the populace with a nationalist cause to hang on to:

> "When at last the Foreign Devils
> Are expelled to the very last man,
> The Great Qing, united, together,
> Will bring peace to our land."

The anti-Christian campaign began with pillage but quickly degenerated into murder. By early June of 1900 various bands of Boxers — some in yellow turbans and red leggings and with charms dangling from their wrists — had reached Beijing. Worried Western powers had sent an extra four hundred men to protect their nationals and, when the Boxers tore up train tracks and telegraph wires, another two thousand soldiers were despatched

ÉVÉNEMENTS DE CHINE
Une victoire française

from the garrison at the treaty port of Tianjin. Unfortunately they suffered heavy losses against the Boxers and retreated. The allied troops then retook the Dagu Forts at the mouth of the river at Tianjin, in readiness for another assault.

Within the Forbidden City, the empress dowager held an emergency meeting with her officials. Realizing that ultimately the Qing dynasty depended for its survival on the loyalty of the Chinese people, on June 21, 1900 Cixi declared war on the foreign powers. From then on the foreign diplomats and their families in Beijing retreated into a stronghold made up of several adjacent legations, where they were to remain trapped for the following fifty-six days. At the same time the Chinese Christians — suffering even worse casualties than the foreigners — took refuge in the Catholic Cathedral, Beitang.

Relief arrived on August 15, 1900 when twenty thousand allied soldiers marched into Beijing. As the foreigners reached the city, Cixi was rudely interrupted while combing her hair by a bullet through her window. The following day she was on the road with the emperor and a small retinue to Xian, where the court established a temporary capital. Once again, China suffered badly: among other exactions she was forced to pay 450 million taels for the loss of two hundred lives and damage to property.

With the court in Xian, the Forbidden City became the headquarters for the foreign troops. When Cixi returned in 1902, at the precise hour appointed by her astrologer, lining the battlements of

(Left) Cover picture of a periodical showing French victory over the Boxer rebels. (Right) Imperial retinue on the road to Xian.

the Forbidden City were men and women from the foreign legations — a potent symbol of the helplessness to which one of the world's proudest nations had succumbed.

THE LAST ENTHRONEMENT

The deathbed edict of the empress dowager was brought to the mansion of Prince Chun on November 13, 1908. Before the messenger, a grand councilor, had even finished reading it out, the house was in an uproar. The old lady of the house, hearing that her grandson was to accede to the dragon throne vacated by the emperor Guangxu, fainted away in shock. Servants and eunuchs, rushing to her aid, calling for the doctor and serving tea to the august visitor, only added to the confusion. At that moment the boy started howling, and was only pacified when his wet-nurse gave him the breast.

And so this frightened child, barely three years old, found himself being taken to the Forbidden City, away from his mother whom he would not see again for seven years, and enthroned as the Son of Heaven.

"Two days after I entered the palace Tzu Hsi [Cixi] died, and on December 2, the 'Great Ceremony of Enthronement' took place, a ceremony that I ruined with my crying.

"The ceremony took place in the Hall of Supreme Harmony . . . Before it began I had to receive the obeisances of the commanders of the palace guard and ministers of the inner court in the Hall of Central Harmony . . .

and the homage of the leading civilian and military officials. I found all this long and tiresome; it was moreover a very cold day, so when they carried me into the Hall of Supreme Harmony and put me up on the high and enormous throne I could bear it no

(Opposite) Throne room in the Hall of Supreme Harmony. (Above) Two-year-old Puyi on the right, with his younger brother Pujie on the left

longer. My father, who was kneeling below the throne and supporting me, told me not to fidget, but I struggled and cried, 'I don't like it here. I want to go home. I don't like it here. I want to go home.' My father grew so desperate that he was pouring with sweat. As the officials went on kowtowing to me my cries grew louder and louder. My father tried to soothe me by saying, 'Don't cry, don't cry; it'll soon be finished, it'll soon be finished.'"[1]

It *was* soon finished, for less than three

years later a republican revolution swept away the Qing dynasty and more than two millennia of imperial rule. On February 12, 1912 Puyi, the last emperor of China, abdicated.

But to all intents and purposes the ex-emperor simply carried on as before. An extraordinary compromise had been forged with the new government: the Son of Heaven graciously established by imperial decree a change of government and his own abdication; the republican government, gracious in its turn, let the emperor retain all the trappings of his role except political power. Since Puyi was only six years old at the time, the decree was proclaimed in the name of empress dowager Longyu, Guangxu's widow: "The whole nation is now inclined towards a republican form of government. The southern and central provinces first gave clear evidence of this inclination, and the military leaders of the northern provinces have since promised their support to the same cause. By observing the nature of the people's aspiration we learn the Will of Heaven. We should not withstand the desires of the nation merely for the sake of the glorification of Our own House. We recognise the signs of the age, and We have tested the trend of popular opinion; and We

now, with the Emperor at Our side, invest the nation with the sovereign power, and decree the establishment of a constitutional government on a republican basis."[2]

At the same time that the abdication was negotiated, another document was drawn up, the Articles of the Favorable Treatment of the Great Qing Emperor after His Abdication, which granted the imperial house an annual stipend and allowed it to retain property, titles, bodyguards, attendants (though no more eunuchs would be engaged), and the inner palaces of the For-bidden City as "temporary accommodation," prior to the court's removal to the summer palace of Yiheyuan (the Garden for Cultivating Harmony) in the outskirts of Beijing.

Although Puyi was forced to withdraw to the Inner Court, leaving the Three Front Halls to be requisitioned by the republican nationalist government, he kept all his privileges. On certain days he still held court, with his kinsmen and officials coming to the Palace of Heavenly Purity in all their finery to make their kowtows in a replay of the grand audiences that used to be held in the Hall of Supreme Harmony. Only now make-believe had completely taken over the reality.

It was in the Palace of Heavenly Purity that Puyi married his empress Wanrong (the

In the Imperial Garden, Puyi on far right with his tutor Reginald Johnston on far left.

poor lady who became addicted to opium) and his consort Wenxiu in a double wedding on the same day in December 1922. Puyi was entering married life during a period of alarming uncertainty. Any hope that he and his wives could quietly pass the rest of their lives as pensioners of the republic was simply doomed. The empire had crumbled, but the government that replaced it seemed to be falling apart as well. Hapless in a world in which he had become irrelevant, Puyi felt insecure about his political position, his entitlement to favorable treatment promised by the Articles, and his own safety even inside the Forbidden City. A way out, he thought, would be to throw himself upon the mercy of the foreign envoys in the capital's Legation Quarter and eventually to go abroad, perhaps to study at an English university. His English tutor Reginald Johnston had, after all, encouraged this idea.

Puyi laid his plan of escape well. To ensure that as a private citizen he would be rich enough still to lead a life of luxury, he began helping himself to the most valuable treasures of the imperial collection. No one was very clear about their ownership in any case. Did they still belong to Puyi, though he

had abdicated? Or had they become the property of the republic? The Articles of Favorable Treatment had formally acknowledged that Puyi's private property would be safeguarded; equally, there was an agreement covering the sale of those treasures to the nation, though in the event the republican government could not raise the

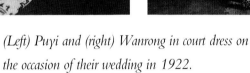
(Left) Puyi and (right) Wanrong in court dress on the occasion of their wedding in 1922.

money to pay for them. Playing on this ambiguity, Puyi, with the help of his brother Pujie, picked hundreds of rare books and more than a thousand scrolls of painting and calligraphy to put by for a rainy day. Some of these treasures were sold when later he found himself exiled to Tianjin, but most of them were to follow him to Manchuria, where,

propped up by the Japanese, he became ruler of the puppet state of Manchukuo in 1932.

Selling off pieces from the imperial collection was also a source of income for the court, which all too often found its expenditure exceeding the annual stipend. We hear of dealers being invited into the palace to bid for gold plate, jewels, porcelain and the like, and of the imperial house securing bank loans by putting up valuable antiques as collateral. The collection was further diminished through theft by servants and officials: Puyi described it as "an orgy of looting".[1]

Puyi's scheme to escape abroad was thwarted by those around him, including his father Prince Chun. Frustrated, he turned his attention to the chaotic court, and one day in 1923 ordered an inventory to be taken of treasures stored in a disused part of the Forbidden City, the Palace of Established Happiness (Jianfugong) and the pavilions in its garden. But no sooner had he given his order than a fire broke out in one of those pavilions, destroying in a matter of hours the entire garden and all the treasures stored there. The cause of the fire remains a mystery: was it arson or an accident? Puyi suspected the former,

(Above) The Jesuit Cemetery in Beijing. (Below right) Casket containing Puyi's ashes, at Babaoshan. (Following page) The mausoleum of emperor Qianlong.

claiming that eunuchs had deliberately set fire to the pavilions to avoid discovery of their looting. But circumstantial evidence suggests that it could equally well have been an accident triggered by an electrical fault.

The fire was a final blow to the eunuchs; almost to a man, they were dismissed by Puyi and expelled from the palace. But time was running out for Puyi too. Dark clouds were gathering — there was civil strife among militarists and warlords fighting to take charge of the country, and there would be Japanese aggression, the emergence of communism, a proletarian revolution. In November 1924 Feng Yuxiang, a general of the National Army, gained control of the capital city after a *coup d'état*. Puyi recalled looking out at Prospect Hill through a telescope from the Imperial Garden and seeing that it was swarming with soldiers whose uniforms were different from those of the palace guard. On the same day, while he was sitting in the Palace of Concentrated Beauty with his empress, an envoy from the general came with an ultimatum: a revised Articles of Favorable Treatment which abolished Puyi's titles and required him to leave the Forbidden City forthwith. Reginald Johnston later described the humiliating expulsion on November 5 in some detail, saying that Puyi and Wanrong, accompanied by two or three servants, were allowed to take only a few personal possessions. But Johnston did not mention that as the cars carrying them reached the Gate of Spiritual Valor, palace guards found a priceless work of calligraphy, entitled *Clearing after Snow,* hidden in the luggage and relieved the imperial party of it. Puyi was then driven past Prospect Hill and through one of the side portals of the gate that led out of the Imperial City.

For a sense of conclusion to the saga of the late empire of China, we too should leave the Forbidden City and make for the sprawling grounds outside Beijing, where the tombs of Wanli, Kangxi, Yongzheng, Qianlong and Cixi are to be found. In life they did not neglect the need of posterity to honor the departed, and prepared their final resting place with the same attention to geomantic forces that they gave to their earthly residence. In death they lie in graves untended by descendants. Never in their wildest dreams could they have imagined that in this they would share a fate with the Jesuits who died far away from home — Ricci, Schall, Verbiest, Castiglione — buried in their own cemetery behind what is now the communist party school in Beijing. For twenty-eight years the ashes of Puyi lay not with his ancestors but in the Babaoshan Cemetery for Revolutionary Heroes. They were moved to a grave near the Western Qing Tombs in 1995.

1 Aisin-Gioro Pu Yi: *From Emperor to Citizen*
2 Reginald F. Johnston: *Twilight in the Forbidden City*

FROM PALACE TO MUSEUM

The barriers have tumbled.

The Forbidden City has become a public place:

now everyone strolls freely through its courtyards,

sips tea under its porches; Young Pioneers in red

neckerchiefs visit the exhibits mounted in its

hallways; certain buildings have been turned into

palaces of culture, into libraries; in another part

of it the government has its seat.

Simone de Beauvoir:

The Long March, An Account of Modern China (1958)

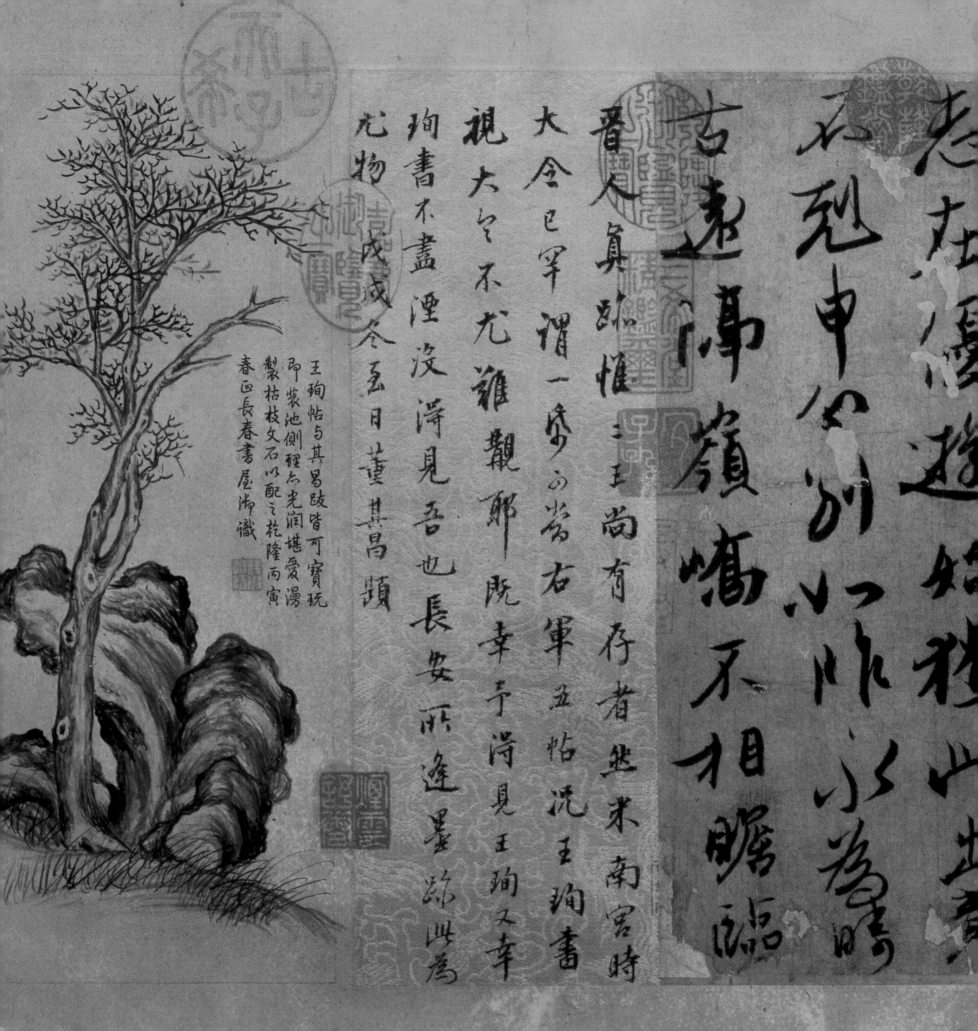

珣頓首頓首
伯遠勝業情期
群從之寶自以羸患
志在優游始獲此出
意不剋申分別如昨永為
古遠隔嶺嶠不相瞻臨

晉尚書令王珣真跡惟
二王尚有存者繇米南宮時
大令已軍謂一帖右軍五帖沉王珣書
視大令不尤雜觀郇既幸于得見王珣又幸
珣書不盡湮沒浮見吾也長安所遇墨跡此為
尤物戊戌冬至日蓮其昌題

王珣帖與其昌跋皆可寶玩
即裝池側裡點光潤堪受湯
製枯枝文石以配之乾隆丙寅
春日長春書屋御識

PRIVATE AND PUBLIC TREASURES

The Qing emperors established two cemeteries in the environs of Beijing, one on the east and one on the west, and it is near the latter that Puyi found his final resting place. For the last emperor, however, there was to be no elaborate tomb hacked out of the side of a mountain or sunk deep underground. His grave is found in the private Hualong cemetery, and no spirit way, stele pavilion or sacrificial hall encompasses it. Instead, clipped hedges of cypresses frame a simple headstone engraved with the characters for "Aisin Gioro Puyi" and the dates "1906–1967", and only two ornamental columns carved with dragons hint at imperial pretensions. Care had been taken, nevertheless, to locate the tomb exactly on a north–south axis, and to ensure that it faces south.

Puyi's tomb was not filled with the sort of funeral objects that would tempt grave robbers, unlike those of his predecessors. In 1928, the tombs of the Qianlong emperor and of the empress dowager Cixi were picked clean by a republican commander and his troops. If one account is to be believed, Qianlong was interred with ingots, books, scrolls of calligraphy and painting, ornaments in jade and ivory, and golden statues of the Buddha; Cixi had lain under heaps of jewels and seventeen strings of pearls, not to mention a dazzling selection of gems strung together as prayer beads.

(Pages 134-35) Scroll from a series, Pictures of Ancient Playthings, by court painters; detail. (Opposite) A detail of the 'Letter to Bo Yuan'. (Above) Puyi's grave in the Hualong cemetery.

The imperial house was robbed time and again; yet, as Jonathan Spence recounts in his Introduction to this book, the Forbidden City (and other imperial residences) had filled with such a wild profusion of loot, tribute gifts and the creations of China's finest artists and craftsmen that the theft and ravages hardly showed. The core of the palace collections, says Spence, "remained virtually intact in all their astonishing variety."

China's emperors had collected art and rare and precious things since very early times. For them, as for other patrons then and now, collecting antiques not only reconnected them with the glorious past, it was also a way of accentuating their wealth, status, power and taste. Ritual and ceremonial objects in precious materials were especially compelling symbols of power and authority, and no worthy collection would be without a number of ancient bronze vessels or jade carvings. In the Tang dynasty (618–907), when Buddhism became firmly entrenched in Chinese culture, religious iconography and tomb frescoes flourished. The Song dynasty (960–1127) inherited a great artistic tradition from the Tang, and its numerous masters went on to perfect landscape painting, many of which were executed for the court. The Song emperor Huizong (r. 1101–25), himself a superb calligrapher, established the first academy of painting in

China. He not only involved himself in the teaching, he also attended to the acquisition of paintings for its gallery. Huizong's own collection of more than six thousand paintings included the fifth- to sixth-century scroll known as the *Admonitions of the Instructress to the Court Ladies,* which would eventually be acquired by Qianlong.

The imperial collection was constantly added to, of course, with specially commissioned works from contemporary artists and craftsmen. These would include portraits of the emperors themselves (see page 110), and scrolls that recorded momentous events in their reigns: a wedding (see page 32), for example, or a victorious battle (see pages 100-101). Wealth and rank were just as clearly expressed through luxury objects, demand for which stimulated extensive development of the decorative arts. The imperial family ate off the finest porcelain, wore silks embellished by the most intricate embroidery, and kept thousands of decorated curios and ornaments for their private study and enjoyment. Eventually those objects themselves would come to be admired as artistic works of rare beauty. Song-dynasty ceramics, for instance, were prized by collectors in the Ming and Qing, just as Ming porcelain wares would become collectors' items as time went on.

江山千里望
無限元氣淋
滿運以神北
宋院誠鮮二
本三唐法從
并多效可驚
嘗世王和趙
己評一堂君
吾臣昌不自
思作人者尒
時調鼎作何
人
丙午新正月
御題

A Thousand Miles of Rivers and Mountains (Qianli jiangshan): detail of a scroll by Wang Ximeng, Song dynasty.

By the Qing dynasty, the imperial collection, its core made up of those bronzes, jades, calligraphy and paintings from antiquity, had become a tangible testimony to a brilliant and long-lived civilization, and to the collectors' claim of being rightful inheritors and guardians of that civilization. It was vastly expanded by the three outstanding emperors of the Qing: Kangxi, Yongzheng and Qianlong.

Kangxi, the second Manchu to rule China, ascended the throne when he was seven years old. As a boy, he learnt written Chinese in secret, taking his lessons from two old eunuchs at court. As a young man, he studied the Confucian classics, and his patronage of scholarship and Chinese culture was most conspicuous in a number of literary and publishing projects, notably a sweeping 5,000-volume encyclopedia (*Qinding gujin tushu jicheng*), an anthology of Tang poems, and the *Kangxi Dictionary*.

He was equally conscientious about supporting the fine arts. To his court came such painters as Giuseppe Castiglione, Leng Mei (see page 105) and Wang Hui (see page 91); from the office that supervised the palace workshops, exquisite artifacts in gold, jade, lacquer, bronze, ivory, glass and enamel flowed out to adorn the halls of the Forbidden City.

More assured than his father Kangxi in engaging with Chinese culture, and much less ostentatious than his son (the future emperor Qianlong), Emperor Yongzheng probably had the best aesthetic taste of the three. His delight in the relics of old, a selection of which are charmingly set out in pictorial catalogs in the form of handscrolls (see pages 134–35), was a quiet, almost private, indulgence. Here were the ancient bronzes, the craved jades, the miniature ornaments on their wooden stands. Here also were the delicate porcelain dishes, their bright cobalt blue glaze echoed in an earlier painting, one of the twelve portraits of beautiful women in their private quarters (see page 72, right) commissioned by Prince Yinzhen in 1709–23, before he became the Yongzheng emperor. The beautiful woman in this portrait is veritably surrounded by antiques — including a cobalt blue bowl — and all of them are displayed to graceful effect on the table and in the latticed shelves around her. Yongzheng's patronage

Assembled Blessings, by the Jesuit court painter Giuseppe Castiglione.

extended to the Jesuit artists too. Throughout his reign, Castiglione was creating some of his best work, several of which have remained in the Palace Museum collections in Beijing and Taiwan, such as *Assembled Blessings* and *The Pine, Hawk and Glossy Ganoderma.*

Qianlong might have renounced any interest in "ingenious articles" in his letter to King George III of England, but no other monarch came close to him in his "omnivorous fondness for collecting art."[1] Unlike his grandfather Kangxi, he was formally educated by highly learned academicians in the palace schoolroom and prided himself on his intellectual bent, claiming that in his heart of hearts he was a scholar. Out of the study of the Chinese classics came his profound appreciation of the rich heritage which, though it had been annexed by conquest, was nevertheless now assumed by the Manchu emperors as their own. Qianlong certainly collected a great many ancient bronzes, perhaps the most powerful emblems of political legitimacy.

Deep in the Inner Court, within the Hall of Mental Cultivation, is a small side-

The Pine, Hawk and Glossy Ganoderma, by Castiglione.

chamber named the Hall of Three Rarities — the three rarities being *Clearing after Snow* from the brush of Wang Xizhi, *Mid-autumn Letter* by Wang Xianzhi and *Letter to Bo Yuan* (see page 136) in the hand of Wang Xun, scripts which Qianlong prized above all the calligraphic works in his possession. His pursuit of rare treasures was equally keen in the case of the *Admonitions* scroll, owned by Emperor Huizong as we saw above, and, after passing through various private hands, acquired by Qianlong. Under the rubric "Reunion of Four Beauties", the *Admonitions* scroll together with three other ancient paintings were placed in a favorite garden pavilion attached to the Palace of Established Happiness.

It was not to remain so safely stored away. The fate of the *Admonitions* scroll recalls that of many other imperial treasures, for it was to fall into the hands of looters and end up in the British Museum. The spoils of war have filled many a museum; a large number of the imperial treasures of China that went into private and public collections in the West were plundered after the sack of Yuanmingyuan in 1860, and at the end of the Boxer rebellion in 1900.

One eyewitness of the burning of the Yuanmingyuan summer palace, the Reverend who admitted to "a pang of sorrow" over the destruction, had a great deal to say about the frenzied looting that ensued, blaming the French troops for being worse offenders than the British. General Montauban, commander of the French troops, had claimed that "nothing had been touched." Yet, wrote the Reverend M'Ghee, "it was passing strange that he could not have seen that his own camp outside the palace-gate was blazing with silk of every hue, and the richest embroidery; nor did he know that, at the same moment, you could buy a richly-jewelled watch, enamelled and set round with pearls or brilliants, or with both, for five or six and twenty dollars."[2] The British were more methodical, consolidating the booty, organizing auctions and dividing the prize money among the officers and soldiers.

It was the same story in 1900. In mid-August the combined contingents of Britain, the United States, France, Germany, Japan, Russia, Italy and Austria — the "eight-power allied forces" — had advanced to Beijing to rescue the besieged foreigners in the legation quarter; looting broke out within days of the relief. Field Marshal Count von Waldersee, commander-in-chief of the allied forces, later observed: "Every nationality accords the palm to some other in respect to the art of plundering, but it remains the fact that each and all of them went in hot and strong for plunder."[3] A Dutch diplomat recorded: "When I entered the gate of the British Legation . . . [an] auction was in full swing . . . in front of the Minister's house. A collection of Chinese things lay spread out on the tiled floor, from silks and furs to blackwood furniture and antique bronzes. All the Legation people, amongst them Lady MacDonald [wife of Sir Claud MacDonald, the British Minister in

Peking] sitting on a chair, and a number of other English men and women thronged around this display of valuable articles, taking them up and examining them and discussing their age and merits. . . A sergeant held up each article in turn, and the bidding was lively, but the prices were low, there was evidently a glut in the market. An officer noted down all the sums in a register, the proceeds going to his regiment's prize fund. While this was going on two Chinese mule carts drove in escorted by some Indian soldiers under an officer. They were heavily loaded with more Chinese valuables destined for auction. This had a bad influence on the bidding."[4] Many of the lots eventually found their way to salerooms in London and Paris.

The denizens of the Forbidden City were themselves no less efficient at dispersing the imperial collection. Apart from theft, relics were discreetly disposed of to dealers in the city or placed with banks as security for loans and, when not redeemed, sold to collectors. Sir Percival David's famous ceramics collection in London, for example, was founded on his purchase of imperial porcelain.

By the time Puyi left the Forbidden City in 1924, the Outer Court had already been turned into government offices, and two of the buildings at the side — the Hall

CURIOSITY-STREET, PEKIN.—FROM A SKETCH BY OUR SPECIAL ARTIST.—SEE PAGE 147.

Many imperial relics found their way to dealers and antique shops in the city.

of Martial Valor (Wuyingdian) and the Hall of Literary Brilliance (Wenhuadian) — were being used to exhibit a few of the works of art in the imperial collection.

And with the departure of the imperial family, the northern half of the Forbidden City could be opened as well. Working against the clock, a committee began the Herculean task of making an inventory of the treasures and turning the Forbidden City into a museum, formally inaugurating it as the Palace Museum on October 10, 1925.

Management of the museum in the early years was fraught with difficulty, for when the country was being ravaged by civil war and economic chaos, only perfunctory attention could be paid to the former palace. By the time the English writer Peter Quennell visited it in the early 1930s, much of the glory of the Forbidden City had already been wiped out by those years of neglect: "An awful vacuum seemed to exist through the whole palace. Latticed casements, in the pavilions and under the cloisters, showed black holes where the paper panes were torn. Peering in, one saw dirt and piles of rubbish. The sagging doors were roughly stamped by an official seal.

"Utter emptiness as in a splendid deserted hive: and the sense of squalor which always accompanies such desertion. Something in the atmosphere of a palace

or temple starts to putrefy when the human occupants vanish. And they had all gone; a lounging soldier at the gate . . . watched the foreign intruders with vague insolence. A spectacled person sold tickets from a box; an aged dwarf came toddling up to tear the counterfoils . . . *Sic transit.* The tag slips out so easily; there was a time when the past glories of the world went up in smoke at the touch of change. Nowadays we are more conservative of fallen splendour and empty palaces, from Peking to Madrid, are handed over to a dim rabble of custodians who punch tickets, jingle coins and erect notice boards."[5]

In 1933, just a step ahead of the Japanese army, then advancing from territory it had captured in the northeast of China, the finest treasures of the Forbidden City were packed into 14,000 crates and sent south for security. In the dead of a February night, the first batch, filling eighteen sealed railway carriages, was secretly transported by a zigzag route via Zhengzhou, Xuzhou and the republican capital of Nanjing to the warehouse of a hospital in Shanghai. Over a thousand crates of archival documents, however, remained in Nanjing. Through the next three months, more endangered treasures were evacuated, first to Shanghai and, when storage facilities were built at the Chaotian Palace there in 1936, to Nanjing.

No sooner were the treasures safely consolidated in Nanjing than they had to move again: they were to remain in exile from their original home for fourteen years. When the Sino-Japanese war broke out in 1937, Chiang Kai-shek and the republican army retreated westward to the mountain city of Chongqing, and the treasures followed. Thus began an odyssey, or rather three odysseys — for the treasures were split and moved by different routes — which would end only in 1947, when they were restored to Nanjing. Throughout this epic flight, the treasures remained vulnerable. At Nanjing, for example, while the crates were waiting to be loaded on board a Yangzi River ship run by the British firm Butterfield &

(Above left) Treasure chests stored in a warehouse in Taiwan, 1952. (Below) Transporting treasures by truck and barge between Hanzhong and Chengdu, 1938.

Swire, enemy aircraft strafed the docks. In Hanzhong, the accidental detonation of a hand grenade destroyed two crates containing porcelain from the Qianlong period. There were also lucky escapes. Once, a truck tipped over the edge of a bridge into the river below; its cargo, however, consisted of unbreakable books and documents. Equally fortunate, it was

when Chiang Kai-shek, pressed by the communist forces, withdrew to the offshore island of Taiwan with his troops, some 3,800 crates of treasures went too. This dispersal of the legacy of China's imperial past thus created two Palace Museums — one in Beijing and another in Taipei.

At the Palace Museum in Beijing,

included such masterpieces as two of Emperor Qianlong's calligraphic "rarities", the *Mid-autumn Letter* and *Letter to Bo Yuan*.

One priceless piece of "northeastern commodity" was the Five Dynasties (907–960) scroll *Night Revels of Han Xizai*, snapped up by the painter Zhang Daqian (1899–1983) for 500 taels of gold in Liulichang in the late 1940s. In 1952,

high summer and the river bed was dry. On another occasion, thousands of crates stored in a temple in Emei eluded a fire that swept that county town in 1943.

Hidden in makeshift depositories, schools, temples and caves at several sites in Sichuan province, the treasures miraculously survived the war. For a significant part of the collection, though, the odyssey was not quite over even when Japan surrendered in 1945. In 1948–49,

Wang Shixiang (see page 77) was one of several curators assigned to recover the Forbidden City's dispersed treasures after the Sino-Japanese war, in particular those taken to Manchuria by Puyi, which came to be known as 'northeastern commodities' (*dongbeihuo*) by antique dealers in their Beijing enclave of Liulichang. Other national treasures were either acquired through gift or donation, or retrieved by purchase, many from Hong Kong. These

preparing to leave Hong Kong, where he was living at the time, to settle in South America, Zhang put up a part of his collection for sale. Instead of entrusting it to auction houses, however, he chose to offer the *Night Revels* scroll to China — out of his patriotic concern, it is said, that it would not be lost to a foreign collector. Not only that, but he sold it to the Chinese government for considerably less than its market value.

By then a great clear-up of the Forbidden City had begun. From its silted moat, potholed courtyards, derelict halls and crumbling pavilions, teams of workers swept up tons of weeds, dust, rubbish and windblown sand. Then it was the turn of masons, carpenters and painters, who began the urgent task of repairing and conserving the architecture. Restoration atmosphere for viewing a historical monument. For a museum established in a palace, private mansion, church or temple, there is always a risk that the original character of the building is diminished through its conversion to public use. At the Palace Museum, the curators are all too aware that any wish to preserve the Forbidden City's spirit of imperial

The one fixed point in a rapidly changing China is her architectural and aesthetic legacy; Beijing's Forbidden City and the magnificent collection that lies at the heart of it remain an enduring part of that legacy and a source of inspiration to all who have marveled at them.

Night Revels of Han Xizai by Gu Hongzhong.

has continued ever since, notably in the complete reconstruction of the Garden of the Palace of Established Happiness, destroyed by fire in 1923, and the renovation of the Lodge for Retired Life in Qianlong's Garden (see page 107).

No longer Quennell's "splendid deserted hive", the Palace Museum is today visited by millions and its custodians punch tickets and erect notice boards more than ever, contributing to a less than idyllic grandeur and mystery is inevitably at odds with the aim of presenting a modern museum — one with proper security and safety systems, orderly visitor access and traffic flow, adequate lighting, unobtrusive rest and refreshments areas, and flexible exhibition spaces. But as infrastructure improves, ever greater and better exposure of the halls and pavilions of the Forbidden City should become possible.

1   Alexander Woodside in Willard Petersen (ed.): *The Cambridge History of China Volume 9 Part One*

2   R.J.L. M'Ghee: *How We Got to Peking: A Narrative of the Campaign in China of 1860*

3   Quoted in Diana Preston: *The Boxer Rebellion*

4   William J. Oudendyk: *Ways and By-ways of Diplomacy*

5   Peter Quennell: *A Superficial Journey through Tokyo and Peking*

A MUSEUM MISCELLANY

North of the Palace of Benevolent Tranquility, at the end of a long narrow passage enclosed by high pink walls, is an array of low painted pavilions giving on to small courtyards. In times gone by these were the residences of secondary concubines; today they make up the restoration department of the Palace Museum.

One workshop is entirely devoted to clocks or rather, as the exasperated Jesuit Jean Matthieu de Vantavon described them in 1769, "curious machines and automata." "Automaton" is perhaps the best word to apply to the contraption, being taken apart and repaired in the Palace Museum workshop one recent winter's day: an enamel base, raised on the necks of four gilt horses, supports a mechanical "waterfall" — shimmering slivers of mirror rotating in a vertical movement — and a twirling carousel of gilded shepherdesses with baskets of flowers in the crook of their arms. The small clock at the apex of the waterfall is almost incidental, an afterthought placed there to give the object some purpose. And to leave one in no doubt that this timepiece, for all its blonde shepherdesses and rococo curlicues, once graced a Chinese house, the two words *Da Ji* — "Great Auspiciousness" — are engraved on the base. Yet, contrary to expectations, this nineteenth-century timepiece was made not in a factory in the Imperial City but in Great Britain.

And what is one to make of the cloisonné music box, ornamented with dancing men in European frock coats — one of

whom periodically whirls to the center and opens a scroll ("Fortune and Long Life reaching to the Skies" is inscribed on it) — and topped by a pineapple inlaid with colored glass? This, too, was an imperial possession, but it was the mechanics of Canton who fabricated it.

The emperors Kangxi and Qianlong, amused by such automata, collected thousands of clocks and mechanical toys in their day. But if European clockmakers helped to open the gates of China to the West, Jesuit painters, with their unfamiliar naturalism and their techniques of perspective, were just as welcome. European and Chinese painters, architects and mechanics enjoyed imperial patronage; under Kangxi, the Hall of Fulfilled Wishes (Ruyi Guan) within the Inner Court was set aside as a studio and repair workshop for them.

The Hall of Fulfilled Wishes is no more, but a studio can still be found in the Forbidden City, in the group of courts housing the restoration department of the Palace Museum. We visited it one day. In a room flooded with the cold, intensely bright sunlight of January, restorers were hunched over long red lacquered tables. Two of them cast a last look at their handiwork before rolling it up. Stretched out in front of them was a painting on a scroll, a monumental landscape. It had been cleaned; its backing sheet had been renewed; it had been glued to a wooden board for a whole month so that the creases would fall out; and some rips had been mended. Now all the minute brush strokes were discernible. The original artist had

(Left) French birdcage chiming clock in the collection of the Palace Museum. (Above) Gilded and lacquered clock in the form of a pavilion, made in the Palace workshops. (Page 148) Detail from the scroll of Kangxi's tour of the south.

daubed a network of strokes to build up the foreground of dense dark trees; a narrow brook, depicted in a pale pink wash, could be glimpsed behind the foliage. In the middle ground, wisps of mist, gnarled rocks, and stubbles of vegetation suggested soaring mountains; a tiled roof and a tiny speck of pink on walls defined a hermit's habitation. Above all this loomed gray jagged peaks, climbed by one thin footpath that disappeared into low-hanging clouds. To the naked eye the mending and patching was invisible.

Paper and silk were the raw materials on which images and information were passed down to posterity, and the brush was the indispensable tool for both artist and archivist. Take any memorial from the Historical Archives, and you see rows and rows of crisply brushstroked words, so small and uniform as to resemble print, and so beautifully executed as to be a work of art. The calligraphy is as fresh today as it was when written; the ink has not faded or smudged, nor has the paper decayed.

The imperial archives were placed in the care of the Palace Museum's department of documents in 1925. They were centralized in the First Historical Archives of China, established in 1980 and located in the Forbidden City just inside the West Prosperity Gate. (At the time of writing, the archives were slated to move to a new repository in the west of Beijing in 2010.) Some ten million documents, mostly from the period 1607 to 1940, are in its custody, ranging from decrees, memorials and genealogical records, to menus, playbills and compilations of dynastic history and diaries kept of the emperors' daily activities. They wait to be microfilmed or digitized and comprehensively cataloged. But as this proceeds, some of the documents also need to be painstakingly touched up, repaired and restored. A museum, by definition, tries to arrest the ravages of time. Its work is never-ending.

CHRONOLOGY OF MING AND QING EMPERORS

(Only reign titles are shown)

Ming Dynasty (1368-1644)

Hongwu 洪武	1368-1398	
Jianwen 建文	1399-1402	
Yongle 永樂	1403-1424	
Hongxi 洪熙	1425	
Xuande 宣德	1426-1435	
Zhengtong 正統	1436-1449	
Jingtai 景泰	1450-1456	
Tianshun 天順	1457-1464	

(first reigned as Zhengtong, then resumed government as Tianshun)

Chenghua 成化	1465-1487
Hongzhi 弘治	1488-1505
Zhengde 正德	1506-1521
Jiajing 嘉靖	1522-1566
Longqing 隆慶	1567-1572
Wanli 萬曆	1573-1620
Taichang 泰昌	1620
Tianqi 天啟	1621-1627
Chongzhen 崇禎	1628-1644

Qing Dynasty (1644-1911)

Shunzhi 順治	1644-1661
Kangxi 康熙	1662-1722
Yongzheng 雍正	1723-1735
Qianlong 乾隆	1736-1795
Jiaqing 嘉慶	1796-1820
Daoguang 道光	1821-1850
Xianfeng 咸豐	1851-1861
Tongzhi 同治	1862-1874
Guangxu 光緒	1875-1908
Xuantong (Puyi) 宣統	1909-1911

SELECT BIBLIOGRAPHY

Aisin-Gioro Pu Yi, translated by W.J.F. Jenner. *From Emperor to Citizen* (Foreign Languages Press, Beijing, 1964)

Anderson, Aeneas. *A Narrative of the British Embassy to China in the Years 1792, 1793 and 1794* (J. Debrett, London, 1795)

Arlington, L.C. and Lewisohn, William. *In Search of Old Peking* (Oxford University Press, Hong Kong, 1987)

Beauvoir, Simone de (trans. by A. Wainhouse). *The Long March: An Account of Modern China* (The World Publishing, New York, 1958)

Beeching, Jack. *The Chinese Opium Wars* (Harcourt Brace Jovanovich, San Diego, 1975)

Bell, John. *A Journey from St Petersburg to Pekin 1719-1722*, edited by J.L. Stevenson (Edinburgh University Press, Edinburgh, 1965)

Beurdeley, Cécile and Michel. *Giuseppe Castiglione: A Jesuit Painter at the Court of the Chinese Emperors* (Charles E. Tuttle, Tokyo, 1971)

Birch, Cyril (ed.). *Anthology of Chinese Literature* (Grove Press Inc., New York, 1965)

Blofeld, John. *City of Lingering Splendour: A Frank Account of Old Peking's Exotic Pleasures* (Hutchinson, London, 1961)

Bredon, Juliet. *Peking: A Historical and Intimate Description* (Kelly & Walsh, Shanghai, 1922; Oxford University Press, Hong Kong, 1982)

Cameron, Nigel. *Mandarins and Barbarians: Thirteen Centuries of Western Travelers in China* (John Weatherhill, New York, 1970)

Cao Xueqin, translated by David Hawkes. *The Story of the Stone* (Penguin Books, Harmondsworth, 1973)

Cary-Elwes, Columba. *China and the Cross: Studies in Missionary History* (Longmans, Green & Co., London, 1957)

Chang Hsin-pao. *Commissioner Lin and the Opium War* (Cambridge University Press, Cambridge, 1974)

Collis, Maurice: *The Great Within* (Faber & Faber, London, 1941)

Confucius, translated by James Legge. *Confucius: Confucian Analects, The Great Learning and The Doctrine of the Mean* (Dover Publications Inc., New York, 1971)

Der Ling, Princess. *Two Years in the Forbidden City* (Dodd, Mead and Co., New York, 1924)

Fleming, Peter. *The Siege at Peking* (Hart Davis, London, 1959)

Gallagher, Louis J. (trans.). *China in the Sixteenth Century: The Journals of Matteo Ricci, 1583-1610* (Random House, New York, 1953)

Hibbert, Eloise T. *K'ang Hsi, Emperor of China* (Paul, Trench, Trubner & Co., London, 1940)

Huang, Ray. *1587: A Year of No Significance* (Yale University Press, New Haven and London, 1981)

Huang, Ray. *China: A Macro History* (M.E. Sharpe, Armonk, 1988)

Hummel, Arthur (ed.) *Eminent Chinese of the Ch'ing Period*, 2 vols. (U.S. Government Printing Office, Washington, D.C., 1934-44)

Johnston, Reginald F. *Twilight in the Forbidden City* (Victor Gollancz, London, 1934)

Keswick, Maggie. *The Chinese Garden: History, Art and Architecture* (Rizzoli International Publications, Inc., New York, 1978)

M'Ghee, R.J.L. *How We Got to Peking: A Narrative of the Campaign in China of 1860* (Bentley, London, 1862)

Morse, H.B. *The Chronicles of the East India Company: Trading to China 1635-1834*, 3 vols. (Clarendon Press, Oxford, 1926-29)

Oudendyk, William J. *Ways and By-Ways of Diplomacy* (Peter Davies, London, 1939)

Petersen, Willard (ed.). *Cambridge History of China Volume 9 Part One: The Ch'ing Dynasty to 1800* (Cambridge University Press, Cambridge, 2000)

Peyrefitte, Alain. *The Collision of Two Civilisations* (Harvill/Harper Collins Publishers, London, 1993)

Preston, Diana. *The Boxer Rebellion: The Dramatic Story of China's War on Foreigners that Shook the World in the Summer of 1900* (Walker & Co., New York, 2000)

Quennell, Peter. *A Superficial Journey through Tokyo and Peking* (Faber & Faber, London, 1932)

Seagrave, Sterling. *Dragon Lady: The Life and Legend of the Last Empress of China* (Vintage Books/Random House, Inc., New York, 1993)

Shen Yiling and Jin Yi. *Gongnu tan wang lu* (Zijincheng Chubanshe, Beijing, 1992)

Shurman, Franz and Schell, Orville (eds.).

China Readings 1: Imperial China (Penguin Books, Harmondsworth, 1967)

Singer, Aubrey. *The Lion and the Dragon: The Story of the First British Embassy to the Court of Emperor Qianlong in Peking, 1792-94* (Barrie & Jenkins, London, 1992)

Sirén, Osvald. *The Imperial Palaces of Peking* (Librarie National D'Art et D'Histoire, Paris, 1926)

Spence, Jonathan D. *Chinese Roundabout* (W. W. Norton, New York, 1992)

Spence, Jonathan D. *Emperor of China: Self-Portrait of K'ang-hsi* (Jonathan Cape, London, 1974)

Spence, Jonathan D. *To Change China: Western Advisers in China 1620 to 1960* (Little Brown, Boston, 1969)

Spence, Jonathan D. *The Search for Modern China* (Century Hutchinson, London, 1990)

Spence, Jonathan D. *Ts'ao Yin and the K'ang-hsi Emperor: Bondservant and Master* (Yale University Press, New Haven, 1966)

Staunton, George. *Macartney's Embassy to China* (printed by W. Bulmer & Co., London, 1797 for G. Nicholl, Pall Mall)

Teng, Ssu-yu and Fairbank, John. *China's Response to the West: A Documentary Survey, 1839-1923* (Harvard University Press, Cambridge, 1954)

Waley, Arthur. *The Opium War through Chinese Eyes* (Allen & Unwin, London, 1958)

Wan Qing gongting shenghuo jianwen (Wenshi Ziliao Chubanshe, Beijing, 1982)

Wan Yi, Wang Shuqing and Liu Lu. *Qing dai gongting shi* (Liaoning Renmin Chubanshe, Shenyang, 1990)

Wan Yi, Wang Shuqing and Lu Yanzhen. *Qing dai gongting shenghuo* (The Commercial Press, Hong Kong, 1985)

Wang Shuqing and Li Pengnian. *Qing gong shi shi* (Zijincheng Chubanshe, Beijing, 1991)

Warner, Marina. *The Dragon Empress: Life and Times of Tz'u-Hsi 1835-1908* (Weidenfeld and Nicolson, London, 1972)

Weng, Wan-Go and Yang Boda. *The Palace Museum: Peking* (Orbis Publishing Ltd, New York, 1982)

Willets, William. *Foundations of Chinese Art* (Penguin Books, Harmondsworth, 1958)

Wu, Silas. *Passage to Power: K'ang-hsi and His Heir Apparent 1661-1722* (Harvard University Press, Cambridge, 1979)